The Rise of The Hedge Fund Era

"A new era of newspaper ownership has emerged that has depleted the industry's resources and jeopardizes its future. By the early 2020s, hedge funds—private equity firms that buy out undervalued companies with assets that can be quickly sold for profit—owned a majority of U.S. daily newspapers.

Dr. Qian Yu reveals why the newspaper industry became a target of hedge funds, how hedge fund-owned newspapers are managed and the impact on journalism. The news is not good: hedge fund ownership brings rounds of layoffs, unrealistic financial goals, and cuts in resources to support journalism. She finds newspaper managers cling to their professional values rooted in truth-telling, government vigilance, and public service, but realize their professionalism has little influence in corporate decision-making.

While the digital age has ended public reliance on printed news, Yu chronicles how hedge fund ownership is the greater threat to newspapers' sustainability and their historic roles of community building and informing citizens in a democracy."

—Peter Gade, Ph.D.

"The widespread shift in ownership of U.S. daily newspapers to hedge funds is increasing the economic instability of an industry already under duress in the digital era. Dr. Qian Yu provides the first systematic and in-depth exploration of this change and its impact. Analysis of corporate annual reports provides insight on the vulnerability of newspapers to hedge fund takeover, and in-depth interviews with managers at hedge fund-owned newspapers highlight the severe consequences that ensue after these changes in ownership."

—David Craig, Ph.D.

Qian Yu

The Rise of The Hedge Fund Era

Threats to Journalism and the News Industry

Qian Yu
Eastern New Mexico University
Portales, NM, USA

ISBN 978-3-031-92579-5   ISBN 978-3-031-92580-1 (eBook)
https://doi.org/10.1007/978-3-031-92580-1

© The Editor(s) (if applicable) and The Author(s), under exclusive license to Springer Nature Switzerland AG 2025

This work is subject to copyright. All rights are solely and exclusively licensed by the Publisher, whether the whole or part of the material is concerned, specifically the rights of translation, reprinting, reuse of illustrations, recitation, broadcasting, reproduction on microfilms or in any other physical way, and transmission or information storage and retrieval, electronic adaptation, computer software, or by similar or dissimilar methodology now known or hereafter developed.
The use of general descriptive names, registered names, trademarks, service marks, etc. in this publication does not imply, even in the absence of a specific statement, that such names are exempt from the relevant protective laws and regulations and therefore free for general use.
The publisher, the authors and the editors are safe to assume that the advice and information in this book are believed to be true and accurate at the date of publication. Neither the publisher nor the authors or the editors give a warranty, expressed or implied, with respect to the material contained herein or for any errors or omissions that may have been made. The publisher remains neutral with regard to jurisdictional claims in published maps and institutional affiliations.

Cover Pattern © Melisa Hasan

This Palgrave Macmillan imprint is published by the registered company Springer Nature Switzerland AG.
The registered company address is: Gewerbestrasse 11, 6330 Cham, Switzerland

If disposing of this product, please recycle the paper.

Contents

1 Introduction   1

2 Three Eras of U.S. Newspaper Ownership Patterns   19

3 Journalism Professionalism's New Struggles   49

4 Threats to News Management in the Era of Hedge Fund Ownership   67

5 Methods   93

6 Study One: Results and Discussion   117

7 Study Two: Results and Discussion   135

8 Conclusion   155

Index   165

List of Tables

Table 6.1	Change in operating revenue in observed period	119
Table 6.2	Changes in P/E ratios in observed period	120
Table 6.3	Change in free cash flow in observed period	121
Table 6.4	Change in the number of employees in observed period	123
Table 6.5	Change in employee-related expenses contributed to the total operating expenses during the observed period	124
Table 6.6	Change in the cost value of physical property during the observed period, and the percentage out of the total assets value	125
Table 6.7	Change in the cost value of lands and buildings during the observed period	127
Table 6.8	Corporate transactions of spin-off, merge, and bankruptcy during the observed period	128

1

Introduction

Abstract To introduce the concept of hedge funds to the field of media management in the newspaper industry, it is necessary to explore two key backgrounds. First, conducting an examination of how the newspaper industry has become vulnerable in the market is crucial. Second, it is important to delve into the potential threats that hedge fund ownership might bring to the newspaper industry.

Keywords Hedge funds • Newspaper industry • Ownership • Media management • Publicly traded newspaper

In less than a decade, hedge funds, as active professional equity institutions, have now reached the point where they own a majority of U.S. newspapers (Kim, 2021). This trend has raised concern that hedge funds, as non-media owners motivated exclusively to generate profit, may deny U.S. daily newspapers from fulfilling their professional mission to inform the public in a democracy (Coppins, 2021).

This book is the first to examine the impact of hedge funds on the newspaper industry. Its purpose is to explore how hedge fund ownership affects the U.S. daily newspaper industry and its implications for the democratic mission of journalism. Some research has looked at the concurrent effects of ownership by activist hedge funds in general or in other target industries such as real estate and nursing homes (Morgenson & Rosner, 2023; Stulz, 2007), but none of it has focused on the U.S. daily newspaper industry. This issue only recently caught the attention of the industry when Tribune Publishing was acquired by Alden Global Capital in 2021 (Coppins, 2021). Subsequently, in February 2024, over 200 news staff members from the *Chicago Tribune* and six other newsrooms of Tribune Publishing nationwide went on strike, demanding better pay and retention of 401(k) match benefits (Miller, 2024). While a few studies have investigated the financial impacts of profit margin requirements in the newspaper industry from the stock market (Beam, 2002; Demers, 1996), or the effects of private investors on media management decisions (Lacy et al., 1996; Picard, 2006; Soloski, 2013), none of them have specifically addressed the influence of hedge fund ownership.

The impacts of hedge funds are worthy of study due to their unique and aggressive motivations, as well as the substantial threats they pose to the sustainability of the companies they acquire. The primary motivation that drives hedge funds to acquire businesses is the short-term monetary return (Gad et al., 2021; Stulz, 2007). Unlike traditional investors who aim to invest in healthy and sustainable businesses (Fernando, 2023), hedge funds are eager to quickly gut the businesses they acquire in order to pay back the high interest and the debt borrowed from their partners or clients and gain immediate profit return (Gad et al., 2021; Morgenson & Rosner, 2023). Additionally, hedge funds usually use a significant amount of debt in their acquisition process and subsequently require the acquired companies to repay the debt (Clarke, 2024). For example, in Alden's $633 million purchase of Tribune Publishing, $278 million is in debt (The NewsGuild-CWA, 2024). In short, the acquisition by hedge funds often hinders the acquired company's ability to thrive and leads to faster failure (Ayash & Rastad, 2021; Brav et al., 2015).

Many publicly traded newspaper companies have been targeted by hedge funds in recent years, primarily because the entire newspaper industry has become vulnerable, especially economically. The U.S. newspaper industry once produced a consistently high profit margin of about 10 to 15 percent during the era of private ownership (1704–1960s)

(Soloski, 2005), aligned with the development of industrialization and the growth of the educated population (Demers, 1996). When newspaper companies started joining the stock market in the 1960s (Demers, 1996; Hollifield, 2012), they received considerable investment from the shareholders and investors, which led their profit margin rise to 20 or 30 percent (Soloski, 2005). Comparatively, the Standard and Poor's 500 (S&P 500) average was 6.5 percent within the same period (through the 1960s and 1980s) (Philosophical Economics, 2014). However, the early twenty-first century witnessed a change in the economic dynamics of the newspaper industry due to the fast-growing digital world, with alternative media emerging and the traditional newspaper business model becoming disrupted, influenced by changes in reading behavior and advertisers' preferences (Picard, 2011). For example, overall newspaper industry revenue (advertising and circulation) fell by 64%, from an estimated $59 billion in 2000 to $21.4 billion in 2022, according to the latest Newspapers Fact Sheet from the Pew Research Center (2023). Today, these public newspaper companies have been targeted by hedge funds for leveraged buyouts and takeovers.

This book will first examine the economic characteristics of newspaper companies that are targeted by hedge funds and which they label as "undervalued." Unlike normal equity institutions that target companies with a healthy and stable economic situation, hedge funds focus on undervalued companies with relatively cheap stock prices but plenty of tangible resources that can be sold off (Stulz, 2007). This allows them to quickly repay the debt and generate profit (Clarke, 2024). Specifically, the price-to-earnings (P/E) ratio is often used to indicate whether a publicly traded company is undervalued or overvalued (Fernando, 2021). For a publicly traded company, a positive free cash flow is an indicator of the ability to maintain a healthy and balanced economic situation, which can come from sources such as operational revenue (i.e., advertising), debt, or loans (Murphy, 2023). The tangible resources that hedge funds primarily focus on are employees and physical properties, which they can quickly gut for immediate profit (Morgenson & Rosner, 2023). Lastly, extreme corporate transactions, such as spin-offs, mergers, or bankruptcies, often expose a company's most vulnerable moments, which could trigger actions from hedge funds (Stulz, 2007).

This book also breaks new scholarly ground by examining how hedge funds' motivation for immediate profit returns can influence news management in the daily newspaper industry, thus extending these impacts to journalism norms in a democracy. Managing knowledge workers, such as journalists, in a knowledge industry like the newspaper sector requires managers to not only clarify the owners' mission but also establish objectives to motivate rank-and-file employees and consider the social impacts of newspapers, as emphasized by Drucker (2008) (also see Gade, 2004). Because hedge fund ownership is solely motivated by short-term profit returns achieved through selling off physical properties and reducing employee counts (Morgenson & Rosner, 2023), it is highly unlikely for news management to sustain management effectively without the support of enough tangible resources and the recognition of professional journalism values. Therefore, hedge funds' harvesting activities in the newspaper companies they acquire may eventually diminish the function of journalism norms that inform citizens well, thus supporting a healthy democratic society.

Vulnerable Newspaper Industry

The newspaper industry's circulation has been declining for four decades, spurred by an increased number of media choices, including cable television and niche media, and its business landscape significantly faltered and became vulnerable when it entered the digital era (Picard, 2011). Many public newspaper companies indicated that their primary competition comes from digital platforms (such as search, aggregation, and social media functionality), instead of from other traditional newspaper companies (i.e. Tribune Publishing annual report, 2020, p. 8; New York Times annual report, 2021, p. 9). Based on a report by the Pew Research Center, almost half (48 percent) of U.S. adults indicate that they frequently obtain news from social media platforms (Walker & Matsa, 2021); correspondingly, U.S. daily newspaper circulation (print and digital combined) fell 54 percent between 2010 and 2022 (Newspapers Fact Sheet, 2023).

In order to keep and increase their online audience, newspaper companies have adapted various digital technologies in their operating activities (Picard, 2011; Gade, 2004; Lowrey & Gade, 2012), such as the publishing procedures of digital media platforms and content management software. It is safe to say, U.S. newspapers have embraced all digitalized technologies (Picard, 2009), from the first Web edition product in 1996 (Nix, 2016) to multimedia product portfolios (Chyi & Ng, 2020; Picard, 2005). Newspaper companies have indeed made some achievements in these digital transformation strategies. For example, a recent analysis of publicly traded newspaper companies revealed that the total estimated revenue from circulation (print and digital) amounted to $11.6 billion in 2022, a decrease of 5 percent from 2021. In 2022, digital advertising constituted 48 percent of newspaper advertising revenue, compared to a mere 17 percent in 2011 (Newspapers Fact Sheet, 2023).

However, the revenue that public newspaper companies gained from the digital world cannot make up for what they lost in the traditional publishing market (Chyi & Ng, 2020; Picard, 2009). The main struggle for public newspaper companies lies in transforming or replacing their broken traditional business models with new ones, rather than simply adapting to digital technologies (Picard, 2011; McDowell, 2011; Kane et al., 2015; Hess et al., 2016). A recent study found that digital subscriber fees contribute only 3 percent of total circulation revenue (Chyi & Ng, 2020). In terms of overall advertising revenue in the U.S. in 2023, the newspaper industry accounted for 2.7 percent of the total, marking a decline from nearly 17.8 percent in 2010 (Newspapers Fact Sheet, 2023). Conversely, internet-based digital media have become the primary medium for advertisers, representing estimated 72 percent of the overall advertising revenue, which reached $245 billion in 2022 (Digital News Fact Sheet, 2023). According to the most recent report, the U.S. newspaper industry generated a total revenue of $21.4 billion in 2022, marking a decline from $21.7 billion in 2021, and this represents the lowest annual revenue for the industry between 2005 and 2022 (Newspapers Fact Sheet, 2023).

Even before hedge funds became interested in the newspaper industry, the industry had gone through a prolonged period of cost controls, centralization of operations and cutbacks (Lacy et al., 1996; Picard & Van

Weezel, 2008). In order to reduce operating expenses, newspaper companies have centralized their departmental functions and tightened the tangible resources across their newspaper chain (Picard & Van Weezel, 2008). In particular, centralization means one content-producing platform for a company's whole newspaper chain nationwide (O'Neill & O'Connor, 2008), and one integrated department would share support for back-office operations, such as clearances, record maintenance, accounting, and so on, throughout the company (Boesman et al., 2015). Reducing tangible resources entails rounds of layoffs, most importantly the elimination of many editors and journalists, as well as the selling off of physical assets like newsrooms, buildings, printing presses, and other operational facilities (O'Connell & Brown, 2019). For example, between 2007 and 2022, DallasNews Corporation sharply downsized its employee number by 81 percent from 3400 in 2007 to 663 in 2022 (A.H. Belo annual report, 2007–2022); in the same time period, Gannett reduced the cost of its physical properties by 88 percent from $2.6 billion in 2007 to $0.3 billion in 2022 (Gannett annual report, 2007–2022).

The aggressive cost control activities also directly impact newsroom investment (Van der Burg & Van den Bulck, 2017) and journalism quality. Overall, based on the data obtained from the Bureau of Labor Statistics' Occupational Employment and Wage Statistics, the number of employees in the newspaper industry working as reporters, editors, and other journalistic content publishers in 2020 fell 12 percent from 2019 and 57 percent from 2004 (Walker, 2021). In particular, fewer local journalists mean some local news beats are no longer covered (O'Neill & O'Connor, 2008), and insufficiently covering local audiences and communities means newspapers can't perform their journalistic professional missions of informing and public service (Lowrey & Woo, 2010). For example, *The Morning Call* (Allentown, Pennsylvania, a local newspaper) no longer regularly covers health, labor, or higher education issues; *Carroll County Times* (Westminster, Maryland, a local newspaper) no longer covers all the municipalities of Carroll County (Davidow, 2020). Moreover, there is much evidence that downsizing resources has harmed journalism quality. For example, the expansion of news deserts occurs as a result of financial constraints and a lack of sufficient local journalists. Many daily newspapers have become ghosts of their former selves (Abernathy, 2023).

According to The State of Local News report, today, two-thirds of the nation's counties do not have a daily newspaper (Abernathy, 2023).

In summary, despite the U.S. newspaper industry's efforts to counteract the negative effects of the digital world, it continues to face vulnerability in terms of its operating performance today. Due to this vulnerability, investing in publicly traded newspaper companies carries a high risk of financial loss, making them a risky investment (Simpson, 2021). Hedge funds, on the other hand, are known for pursuing risky investments as they believe that high risk can lead to high rewards (Clarke, 2024; Tretina & Schmidt, 2022).

Potential Threats Created by Hedge Funds

Hedge funds are opportunistic private investors with an ultimate goal of immediate profit returns (Bratton & McCahery, 2015; Edmonds, 2020). They exhibit a preference for intensive involvement in the corporate governance of their target companies to achieve faster gains (Clarke, 2024; Goltz, 2006). Therefore, when hedge funds acquire ownership in a newspaper company, their aggressive motivations and harvesting activities can pose challenges for professional media managers.

Unlike traditional investors, who prioritize sustainability in their investments, hedge funds are active financial entities often referred to as "money-spinning machines" (Morgenson & Rosner, 2023, p. 2). Their sole objective is immediate profit return through aggressively restructuring the companies they acquire (Stulz, 2007). In this pursuit, hedge funds actively engage in corporate governance, leading to potential conflicts with managers who are aligned with the value-creation processes of the company's former owners (Acharya et al., 2013).

Due to the significant role of ownership in a company, hedge funds may pose a threat to a company's mission and the journalism norms it upholds through their aggressive harvesting actions. Ownership and management are generally interrelated concepts, as owners are responsible for operating their companies through managers (Bansal, 2013; Bryan, 2015; Drucker, 2008). Conceptually, ownership issues emphasize how owners decide the mission and strategy at the firm level, while management issues are the daily things that professionals must do in order to achieve the organization's strategies (Bryan, 2015). Managers use their special knowledge to facilitate owners' organizational mission to run smoothly (Bryan, 2015; Demsetz & Villalonga, 2001). In addition, organizational structural complexity is the trigger point that compels owners to hire managers who possess diverse professional knowledge and skills (Drucker, 2008).

Traditionally, the U.S. newspaper industry has had two main missions: facilitating democracy through high quality of journalism and economic independence through profit-oriented business (Merrill, 2012; Lowrey & Woo, 2010). Being profit-oriented has been perceived as a means of safeguarding independent journalism and maintaining the quality of public service (Demers, 1991, 1996). Private individual and public newspaper owners all operate with these two missions, but have different focuses and motivations. Private individual or family-owned papers are often motivated by their personal issues, such as personal prestige, social influence, etc. (Demers, 1996), so they usually only focus on the community where the owners live and on the local audience's perspectives. Local public service quality is important to them (Meyer, 2009). During 1970–80, newspaper consolidation opened the door for the corporate newspaper ownership, which had greater capabilities to use resources efficiently (Demers, 1996) and more opportunities to get financial support from the capital market (Hollifield, 2012; Albarran, 2023). Many corporate newspapers became publicly traded newspaper companies so they could sell stock to the public (Hollifield, 2012). Moreover, the consistent investment from the stock market can positively support public newspaper companies to spend more on maintaining the quality of journalism and public service than what they did during the private newspaper ownership era that dominated the 1960s (Demers, 1996). For instance, corporate newspapers cover multiple communities or local markets (Demers, 1996), allowing them to embrace more critical and inclusive opinions and cover more complex news topics (Demers, 1996). However, the focus on satisfying investors can have some negative influence on media management. These negative impacts have been noticed with the key idea that active investors indirectly affect companies' outcomes through their actions, such as the level of activism (Bottazzi et al., 2008). Particularly, with reference to the newspaper industry, the presence of financial investors can lead management to make more short-term decisions (Lacy et al., 1996).

In terms of journalism norms, in a democratic society, the functions of journalism should encompass telling the truth, providing information, enlightening the public, and safeguarding the rights of individuals (Siebert et al., 1956). Social responsibility theory emphasizes the importance of journalism in promoting public welfare (Siebert et al., 1963). Furthermore, in practical terms, the role of "quality" journalism requires an adequate number of journalists and local newsrooms to support its function in serving the public interest (Iggers, 2018; Tameling & Broersma, 2013). In the U.S., most newspapers are based in communities (Chyi, 2013), so the quality journalism means enough community coverage (Peters & Broersma, 2013; Abernathy, 2018). However, reducing the number of journalists and selling newspapers' buildings are the core of hedge funds' harvesting actions (Bratton, 2008; Channick, 2021; Stulz, 2007). For example, buyouts were offered to nonunion employees two days after Alden completed its acquisition of Tribune Publishing (Channick, 2021). Moreover, Alden's real estate company, Twenty Lake Holdings, specializes in the efficient acquisition, sale, leasing, and redevelopment of newspaper offices and printing plants (O'Connell & Brown, 2019).

In the context of news management within a complex corporate newspaper company or media chain, managers are often driven by social motivations rather than purely economic incentives (Glinkowska & Kaczmarek, 2015). Previous research has shown that media managers evaluate the value of their work based on the recognition they receive from their peers (Gade, 2004). Additionally, the concept of "approved contradiction" suggests that newspaper managers prioritize professional and organizational objectives while ensuring they generate sufficient profit to meet the expectations of their corporate owners (Galbraith, 1978; Demers, 1996, 1999). However, in the realm of private equity, the relationship between managers and owners is guided by agency theory, which highlights the need for owners to monitor and mitigate managers' self-interests while managers are expected to act in the owners' best interests (Panda & Leepsa, 2017). Conflicts of interest between owners and managers are often viewed as internal expenses known as agency cost (Bratton, 2008). As a result, professional knowledge held by newspaper managers, which was once valued by corporate newspaper owners, may be perceived as agency costs and potentially reduced by hedge funds.

Additionally, one key reason that triggers hedge funds to target publicly traded newspaper companies is their identification of these companies as "undervalued" in the stock market (Edmonds, 2020). "Undervalued" is a financial term referring to when the company's stock price is below its true intrinsic value (Khartit, 2020). To hedge funds, "undervalue" means that it's time to harvest—a "take-the-money-and-run" plan (Meyer, 2009). Hedge funds act when a company experiences a trigger moment, usually an extraordinary, sudden corporate transaction such as a merger, spin-off, or bankruptcy (Stulz, 2007). For example, hedge fund Chatham Asset Management acquired The McClatchy Company right after the newspaper company filed for bankruptcy in 2020 (Hall, 2020), and Alden Global Capital attacked Tribune Publishing when the board's chair stepped down in 2019 and sold his 25 percent stake in the company to Alden (Davidow, 2020).

To evaluate an "undervalued" company, two common indicators are a low Price-to-Earnings ratio (P/E ratio) (Ghaeli, 2016) and negative free cash flow (Bhandari & Adams, 2017). The P/E ratio is a valuation measure used to assess a company, which compares its current share price to its earnings per share (Edmonds, 2020; Szajowski & Łebek, 2007), and it is influenced by both the company's present earnings and its anticipated future earnings (Bass, 1990). A high P/E ratio indicates that a stock's price is high relative to its earnings and possibly overvalued, while a low P/E ratio may signal that the current stock price is low relative to earnings (Ghaeli, 2016). Moreover, free cash flow represents the funds remaining for a company after covering its operating expenses and capital expenditures, and it serves as an indicator of a company's efficiency in generating cash, although this frequently comes from short- or long-term debt or loans (Bhandari & Adams, 2017). Essentially, free cash flow is similar to profit in that they both represent the remaining income. However, the debt or loans must be paid back eventually, whereas profit is what remains in the company's pocket (Murphy, 2023).

This book will examine the impacts of hedge fund ownership on the U.S. daily newspaper industry through two studies. Study One will focus on the factors that attract hedge funds to harvest newspaper companies, specifically focusing on the factors of P/E ratio, free cash flow, tangible resources, and trigger moments formed. A longitudinal study is an observational research technique that involves studying an issue over an extended period (Caruana et al., 2015). This study spanned 16 years that cover the year before the 2008 recession (2007) to the most recent year of annual report published year (2022), as the 2008 recession is a significant watershed in U.S. economic history that prompted many industries, including the newspaper industry, to undergo substantial changes in their business landscapes (Chyi & Tenenboim, 2019). Moreover, the rapid development of the digital media industry caused the newspaper industry to face even more trouble rebounding after the 2008 recession (Picard, 2009). Furthermore, publicly traded newspaper companies' annual reports will be used for analysis. An annual report (10-K form) is the only place where publicly traded companies fully address their corporate strategies to the public (Kenton, 2020; Martin, 1998).

The financial problems examined in Study One provide insights not only into why this entire industry became attractive for hedge funds in the digital age, but also into the concurrent management struggles for news managers during the era of public ownership, such as limited tangible resources. The data analysis results shed light on additional management challenges during the era of hedge fund ownership in Study Two.

Study Two explores news managers' perspectives on the impact of ownership shifting to hedge funds on their daily management work, extending to the question of journalism norms in a democracy. Specifically, this study focused on understanding ownership missions, setting objectives with rank-and-file employees, and maintaining the organizational social impacts (Drucker, 2008). This study employed in-depth interviews with news managers who are currently working for newspaper companies that were acquired by hedge funds. This method enables researchers to collect comprehensive data, allowing participants to articulate and elucidate their opinions (Denzin & Lincoln, 2008).

Together, the two studies offer a picture of how hedge fund ownership impacts the newspaper industry and the democratic mission of journalism.

Additionally, in terms of the research population, a basic consideration is that hedge funds typically specialize in and emphasize specific industries (Stulz, 2007), indicating that when they start targeting a particular public newspaper company, it implies that all public newspaper companies have become potential targets. Hedge funds tend to target a single industry in order to concentrate their expertise, resources, and experience, enabling them to govern efficiently and predictably (Hartzell & Starks, 2003).

Therefore, newspaper companies that have been targeted or are currently owned by hedge funds are valuable to study and analyze as an alert for the entire newspaper industry. Specifically, for Study One—content analysis of annual reports—the research population includes Gannett (i.e., *USA Today*), Lee Enterprises (i.e., *Buffalo News*), Tribune Publishing (i.e., *Chicago Tribune*) and McClatchy (i.e., *Miami Herald*). The first two newspaper companies experienced fierce attacks by hedge funds but managed to survive, while the latter two newspaper companies were recently acquired by hedge funds. For Study Two—in-depth interview with news managers—potential interviewees were sought from Tribune Publishing and McClatchy, which are currently under the full control of hedge fund ownership. This will allow news managers to offer direct perspectives about the impacts of hedge fund ownership on newspapers.

References

Abernathy, P. M. (2018). *The expanding news desert*. Center for Innovation and Sustainability in Local Media, School of Media and Journalism, University of North Carolina at Chapel Hill.

Abernathy, P.M. (2023, November). More than half of U.S. counties have no access or very limited access to local news. Northwestern Medill. https://www.medill.northwestern.edu/news/2023/more-than-half-of-us-counties-have-no-access-or-very-limited-access-to-local-news.html

Albarran, A. B. (2023). *The media economy*. Routledge.

Acharya, V. V., Gottschalg, O. F., Hahn, M., & Kehoe, C. (2013). Corporate governance and value creation: Evidence from private equity. *The Review of Financial Studies, 26*(2), 368–402.

Ayash, B., & Rastad, M. (2021). Leveraged buyouts and financial distress. *Finance Research Letters, 38*, 101452.

Bansal, P. (2013). Inducing frame-breaking insights through qualitative research. *Corporate Governance: An International Review, 21*(2), 127–130.

Bass, B. M. (1990). From transactional to transformational leadership: Learning to share the vision. *Organizational Dynamics, 18*(3), 19–31.

Beam, R. A. (2002). Size of corporate parent drives market orientation. *Newspaper Research Journal, 23*(2–3), 46–63.

Bhandari, S. B., & Adams, M. T. (2017). On the definition, measurement, and use of the free cash flow concept in financial reporting and analysis: a review and recommendations. *Journal of Accounting and Finance, 17*(1), 11–19.

Boesman, J., d'Haenens, L., & Van Gorp, B. (2015). Triggering the News Story: Reconstructing reporters' newsgathering practices in the light of newspaper type, newsroom centralization, reporters' autonomy, and specialization. *Journalism Studies, 16*(6), 904–922.

Bottazzi, L., Da Rin, M., & Hellmann, T. (2008). Who are the active investors?: Evidence from venture capital. *Journal of Financial Economics, 89*(3), 488–512.

Bratton, W., & McCahery, J. A. (Eds.). (2015). *Institutional investor activism: Hedge funds and private equity, economics and regulation*. OUP Oxford.

Bratton, W. W. (2008). Private equity's three lessons for agency theory. *European Business Organization Law Review (EBOR), 9*(4), 509–533.

Brav, A., Jiang, W., & Kim, H. (2015). Recent advances in research on hedge fund activism: Value creation and identification. *Annual Review of Financial Economics, 7*, 579–595.

Bryan, R. (2015, February). Management vs. ownership. *Greenhouse Management.* https://www.greenhousemag.com/article/gm0215-management-wnership-issues/

Caruana, E. J., Roman, M., Hernández-Sánchez, J., & Solli, P. (2015). Longitudinal studies. *Journal of thoracic disease, 7*(11), E537.

Channick, R. (2021, May). Tribune Publishing offering buyouts to newsroom employees, two days after purchase by hedge fund Alden. *Chicago Tribune.* Retrieved from: https://www.chicagotribune.com/business/ct-biz-tribune-publishing-newsroom-buyouts-alden-20210526-ihthwykitjfmrpnj63whhlqw5i-story.html

Chyi, H. (2013). *Trial and error: US newspapers' digital struggles toward inferiority*. Servicio de Publicaciones de la Universidad de Navarra.

Chyi, H. I., & Ng, Y. M. M. (2020). Still unwilling to pay: An empirical analysis of 50 US newspapers' digital subscription results. *Digital Journalism, 8*(4), 526–547.

Chyi, H. I., & Tenenboim, O. (2019). Charging more and wondering why readership declined? A longitudinal study of US newspapers' price hikes, 2008–2016. *Journalism Studies, 20*(14), 2113–2129.

Clarke, C. (2024, February). Hedge fund definition, examples, types, and strategies. *Investopedia.* https://www.investopedia.com/terms/h/hedgefund.asp

Coppins, M. (2021, October). A secretive hedge fund is is gutting newsrooms. *The Atlantic.* https://www.theatlantic.com/magazine/archive/2021/11/alden-global-capital-killing-americas-newspapers/620171/

Davidow, S. (2020, May). The state of journalism at Tribune publishing. *The NewsGuild.* https://newsguild.org/the-state-of-journalism-tribune-publishing/

Demers, D. (1996). Corporate newspaper structure, editorial page vigor, and social change. *Journalism & Mass Communication Quarterly, 73*(4), 857–877.

Demers, D. (1999). Corporate newspaper bashing: Is it justified? *Newspaper Research Journal, 20*(1), 83–97.

Demers, D. P. (1991). Corporate structure and emphasis on profits and product quality at US daily newspapers. *Journalism Quarterly, 68*(1-2), 15–26.

Demsetz, H., & Villalonga, B. (2001). Ownership structure and corporate performance. *Journal of Corporate Finance, 7*(3), 209–233.

Denzin, N. K., & Lincoln, Y. S. (2008). Introduction: The discipline and practice of qualitative research.

Digital News Fact Sheet. (2023). *Pew research center.* Retrieved from: https://www.pewresearch.org/journalism/fact-sheet/digital-news/

Drucker, P. (2008). Introduction: Management and managers defined; management as a social function and liberal art; knowledge is all. *Management,* 1–25.

Edmonds, R. (2020, July). Alden buyouts have eliminated more than 10% of Tribune Publishing newsroom staffing in just six weeks. *Pointer.* https://www.poynter.org/locally/2021/alden-buyouts-have-eliminated-more-than-10-of-tribune-publishing-newsroom-staffing-in-just-six-weeks/

Fernando, J. (2021, November). Price-to-Earnings (P/E) ratio. *Investopedia.* https://www.investopedia.com/terms/p/price-earningsratio.asp

Fernando, J. (2023, March). Equity for shareholders: How it works and how to calculate it. *Investopedia.* https://www.investopedia.com/terms/e/equity.asp

Gad, S., Scott, G., & Jackson, A. (2021, April). Guide to hedge funds. *Investopedia.* https://www.investopedia.com/articles/investing/102113/what-are-hedge-funds.asp

Gade, P. J. (2004). Newspapers and organizational development: Management and journalist perceptions of newsroom cultural change. *Journalism & Communication Monographs, 6*(1), 3–55.

Galbraith, J. K. (1978). On post Keynesian economics. *Journal of Post Keynesian Economics, 1*(1), 8–11.

Ghaeli, M. R. (2016). Price-to-earnings ratio: A state-of-art review. *Accounting, 3*(2), 131–136.

Glinkowska, B., & Kaczmarek, B. (2015). Classical and modern concepts of corporate governance (Stewardship Theory and Agency Theory). *Management, 19*(2), 84.

Goltz, F. (2006, November). Hedge funds as risk reducers. *IPE.* https://www.ipe.com/hedge-funds-as-risk-reducers/19973.article

Hall, K. (2020, August). Bankruptcy judge approves the sale of McClatchy to hedge fund Chatham Asset Management. *McClatchy.* https://www.mcclatchydc.com/news/nation-world/national/article244710217.html

Hartzell, J. C., & Starks, L. T. (2003). Institutional investors and executive compensation. *The Journal of Finance, 58*(6), 2351–2374.

Hess, T., Matt, C., Benlian, A., & Wiesböck, F. (2016). Options for formulating a digital transformation strategy. *MIS Quarterly Executive, 15*(2).

Hollifield, A. (2012). Changing perceptions of organizations. *Changing the news: The forces shaping journalism in uncertain times*, 193–212.

Iggers, J. (2018). *Good news, bad news: Journalism ethics and the public interest.* Routledge.

Kane, G. C., Palmer, D., Phillips, A. N., Kiron, D., & Buckley, N. (2015). Strategy, not technology, drives digital transformation. *MIT Sloan Management Review and Deloitte University Press, 14*(1–25).

Kenton, W. (2020, March). 10-K. *Investopedia.* https://www.investopedia.com/terms/1/10-k.asp

Khartit, K. (2020, December). Undervalued. *Investopedia.* https://www.investopedia.com/terms/u/undervalued.asp

Kim, S. (2021, June). How hedge funds took over America's struggling newspaper industry. *CNBC.* https://www.cnbc.com/2021/06/11/how-hedge-funds-took-over-americas-struggling-newspaper-industry-.html

Lacy, S., Shaver, M. A., & Cyr, C. S. (1996). The effects of public ownership and newspaper competition on the financial performance of newspaper corporations: A replication and extension. *Journalism & Mass Communication Quarterly, 73*(2), 332–341.

Lowrey, W., & Gade, P. J. (2012). *Changing the news.* Routledge.

Lowrey, W., & Woo, C. W. (2010). The news organization in uncertain times: Business or institution? *Journalism & Mass Communication Quarterly, 87*(1), 41–61.

Martin, H. J. (1998). Measuring newspaper profits: Developing a standard of comparison. *Journalism & Mass Communication Quarterly, 75*(3), 500–517.

McDowell, W. S. (2011). The brand management crisis facing the business of journalism. *The International Journal on Media Management, 13*(1), 37–51.

Merrill, J. (2012). Journalism and democracy. *Changing the news: The forces shaping journalism in uncertain times*, pp. 45–62.

Meyer, P. (2009). *The vanishing newspaper: Saving journalism in the information age.* University of Missouri Press.

Miller, V. (2024, February). Chicago Tribune reporters, newsroom staff strike for first time in newspaper's 180-year history: 'This is Chicago, we don't back down.' *Chicago Sun-Times.* https://chicago.suntimes.com/business/2024/2/1/24058233/chicago-tribune-strike-alden-global-capital-union-walkout-labor-history

Morgenson, G., & Rosner, J. (2023). *These are the plunderers: How private equity runs – And Wrecks – America.* Simon and Schuster.

Murphy, C. (2023, May). Using the price to earnings ratio and PEG to assess a stock. *Investopedia.* https://www.investopedia.com/investing/use-pe-ratio-and-peg-to-tell-stocks-future/

Newspapers Fact Sheet. (2023, November). Pew Research Center. https://www.pewresearch.org/journalism/fact-sheet/newspapers/

Nix, E. (2016, August). The world's first web site. *History. com.* https://www.history.com/news/the-worlds-first-web-site#:~:text=On%20August%206%2C%201991%2C%20without,particle%20physics%20lab%20in%20Switzerland

O'Connell, J., & Brown, E. (2019, February). A hedge fund's 'mercenary' strategy: Buy newspapers, slash jobs, sell the buildings. *The Washington Post.* https://www.washingtonpost.com/business/economy/a-hedge-funds-mercenary-strategy-buy-newspapers-slash-jobs-sell-the-buildings/2019/02/11/f2c0c78a-1f59-11e9-8e21-59a09ff1e2a1_story.html

O'Neill, D., & O'Connor, C. (2008). The passive journalist: How sources dominate local news. *Journalism Practice, 2*(3), 487–500.

Panda, B., & Leepsa, N. M. (2017). Agency theory: Review of theory and evidence on problems and perspectives. *Indian Journal of Corporate Governance, 10*(1), 74–95.

Pew Research Center. (2023, November). Newspapers Fact Sheet. https://www.pewresearch.org/journalism/fact-sheet/newspapers/

Peters, C., & Broersma, M. J. (Eds.). (2013). *Rethinking journalism: Trust and participation in a transformed news landscape.* Routledge.

Philosophical Economics. (2014, March). Profit margins: The death of a chart. https://www.philosophicaleconomics.com/2014/03/foreignpm/

Picard, R. G. (Ed.). (2005). *Corporate governance of media companies.* Jönköping Internat.

Picard, R. G. (2006). Capital crisis in the profitable newspaper industry. *Nieman Reports, 60*(4), 10–12.

Picard, R. G. (2009). OMG! Newspapers may not be dead! *The Media Business, 10,* 2009.

Picard, R. G. (2011). *The economics and financing of media companies.* Fordham University Press.

Picard, R. G., & Van Weezel, A. (2008). Capital and control: Consequences of different forms of newspaper ownership. *The International Journal on Media Management, 10*(1), 22–31.

Siebert, F., Peterson, T., Peterson, T. B., & Schramm, W. (1956). *Four theories of the press: The authoritarian, libertarian, social responsibility, and Soviet communist concepts of what the press should be and do* (Vol. 10). University of Illinois Press.

Siebert, F., Peterson, T., & Schramm, W. (1963). *Four theories of the press: The authoritarian, libertarian, social responsibility, and Soviet communist concepts of what the press should be and do.* University of Illinois Press.

Simpson, S. (2021, August). Low-risk vs. High-risk investments: What's the difference? *Investopedia.* https://www.investopedia.com/financial-edge/0512/low-vs.-high-risk-investments-for-beginners.aspx

Soloski, J. (2005). Taking stock redux: Corporate ownership and journalism of publicly traded newspaper companies. *Corporate Governance of Media Companies,* 59–76.

Soloski, J. (2013). Collapse of the US newspaper industry: Goodwill, leverage and bankruptcy. *Journalism, 14*(3), 309–329.

Stulz, R. M. (2007). Hedge funds: Past, present, and future. *Journal of Economic Perspectives, 21*(2), 175–194.

Szajowski, K., & Łebek, D. (2007). Optimal strategies in high risk investments. *Bulletin of the Belgian Mathematical Society-Simon Stevin, 14*(1), 143–155.

Tameling, K., & Broersma, M. (2013). De-converging the newsroom: Strategies for newsroom change and their influence on journalism practice. *International Communication Gazette, 75*(1), 19–34.

The NewsGuild-CWA. (2024, February). Tribune Publishing journalists go on 24-hour strike. https://newsguild.org/tribune-publishing-journalists-go-on-24-hour-strike/

Tretina, K., & Schmidt, J. (2022, February). How to invest in hedge funds. *Forbes*. https://www.forbes.com/advisor/investing/how-to-invest-in-hedge-funds/

Van der Burg, M., & Van den Bulck, H. (2017). Why are traditional newspaper publishers still surviving in the digital era? The impact of long-term trends on the Flemish newspaper industry's financing, 1990–2014. *Journal of Media Business Studies, 14*(2), 82–115.

Walker, M. (2021, July). U.S. newsroom employment has fallen 26% since 2008. *Pew Research Center*. https://www.pewresearch.org/short-reads/2021/07/13/u-s-newsroom-employment-has-fallen-26-since-2008/

Walker, M., & Matsa, K. E. (2021, September). News Consumption Across Social Media in 2021. *Pew Research Center*. https://www.pewresearch.org/journalism/2021/09/20/news-consumption-across-social-media-in-2021/

2

Three Eras of U.S. Newspaper Ownership Patterns

Abstract To understand why hedge fund ownership could pose an existential threat to the newspaper industry, this chapter will initially identify the three eras of newspaper ownership and examine the fundamental concepts that differentiate the roles of owners and managers in each era.

Keywords Private media ownership • Public media ownership • Hedge fund media ownership • The history of newspaper industry • Media management

Due to the unique product—journalism—the study of media business has been widely discussed in the newspaper industry, particularly in relation to uncertain economic circumstances. In a democratic society, journalism exists to emphasize democratic engagement and maintain a meaningful relationship with its citizen audience (Merrill, 2011; Shoemaker & Reese, 2013). Journalists have created and maintained journalism professional values in education and journalism practice and in education (Macdonald, 2006). Therefore, a primary role of news managers is to balance the different motivations between journalists'

© The Author(s), under exclusive license to Springer Nature Switzerland AG 2025
Q. Yu, *The Rise of The Hedge Fund Era*, https://doi.org/10.1007/978-3-031-92580-1_2

professional values and owners' financial demands (Albarran et al., 2018; Gade, 2008; Sylvie & Gade, 2009).

Moreover, owners' motivations have changed due to newspaper ownership patterns shifting. Since 1704 when the first newspaper was published (Bryan & Merrill, 1993), U.S. newspaper ownership patterns have gone through three eras: private individual/family ownership (1704–1960s), public or publicly traded ownership (1960s–2010), and most recently—hedge fund ownership (2010–present).

The roles of owners and management have been broadly studied in the two previous newspaper ownership eras (Demers, 1996; Hollifield, 2012; Picard & Brody, 1997), but little has been studied about the present era—hedge fund ownership—because it has only recently developed. The first documented case of hedge fund acquisition in the newspaper industry was in 2010 when Digital First Media, one of the largest national newspaper publishers in the U.S. (i.e., *Denver Post*), was bought by hedge fund Alden Global Capital (Sydney, 2018). This acquisition took place immediately after Digital First Media claimed bankruptcy (Sydney, 2018). Since then, Alden has accelerated its aggressive actions toward other publicly traded newspaper companies, using Digital First Media as its base and leveraging its media expertise (Channick, 2021). However, the concept of hedge fund newspaper ownership has only recently received widespread attention: In 2021, Alden Global Capital acquired the third largest newspaper publisher, Tribune Publishing, for $630 million (Channick, 2021; Coppins, 2021).

Hedge funds are private equity institutions that employ a strategy of purchasing stocks with the goal of obtaining ownership in target companies, and they often engage in short sales of tangible resources in order to achieve immediate profit returns (Barnier, 2021). Given that hedge funds already own about half of the nation's newspapers (Maher, 2021), how will news managers maintain journalism quality with even scarcer resources and without any interest from their owners? This has become an industry-wide problem and raises another serious concern—that the lack of journalism may harm a democratic society (Merrill, 2011; also see Lowrey & Gade, 2012; Meyer, 2009).

Private Newspaper Ownership Era (Around 1704–1960s)

Newspapers were established as private entities in democratic societies, such as England in the early eighteenth century and later in the U.S. (Bryan & Merrill, 1993), where their primary purpose was to furnish citizens with the necessary information and truth required for freedom and self-governance (Kovach & Rosenstiel, 2021). Particularly in the U.S., in 1704, the postmaster of Boston, John Campbell, used his position to obtain permission to print the Boston *News-Letter*, which became the first true newspaper in North America (Bryan & Merrill, 1993). The first daily paper was the Pennsylvania *Evening Post* in 1783 owned by Benjamin Towne (Picard & Brody, 1997). Twenty years later, daily newspapers were available in most U.S. cities (Demers, 1996).

The rapid expansion of the U.S. newspaper industry in general started in the early nineteenth century and followed the growth of the industrial revolution (Kirchhoff, 2009). The industrial revolution expedited the growth of urban populations, leading manufacturers to seek efficient ways of reaching buyers through advertising, and urban residents required access to information that could navigate them through an increasingly complex society (Demers, 1996). By the mid-nineteenth century, industrialization had firmly taken root in America's northeastern region and major cities (Kirchhoff, 2009). Consequently, newspapers swiftly emerged and established themselves in these urban areas (Demers, 1996; Picard & Brody, 1997).

The newspaper industry maintained a monopoly over news and information until the first half of the twentieth century when broadcast media began to emerge (radio in the 1930s and TV in the 1950s) and gradually gained public acceptance (Bagdikian, 2004; Bass, 1999). In particular, newspapers' domination of the local audience and advertising market brought the industry high profit margins (Demers, 1996). Before 1940, 98 percent of newspapers existed as the only news and information sources published within their markets (Picard & Brody, 1997). Newspapers' traditional business model was also established during the time, which showed that the sale of advertising relied on the number of readers, and approximately 80 percent of total revenue came from advertising, while the remaining 20 percent came from circulation through the 1990s (Lacy & Martin, 2004; Picard, 2005). In short, the newspaper industry experienced rapid and profitable growth throughout the majority of the private ownership era (Demers, 1996; Picard & Brody, 1997).

The concept of private ownership expanded from individual ownership to family ownership as some newspaper companies survived increased competition. As a result, individually owned businesses were able to accumulate great wealth and became family-owned enterprises (Powers et al., 2014). When some private individual newspaper owners grew in influence and profitability, ownership by entrepreneurial individual owners gradually extended to rich families (Picard & Brody, 1997; Underwood, 1995). Many well-known public media groups recognized by name were created by individuals and later owned by families. For instance, McClatchy Company was founded by James McClatchy, who later handed over leadership to his son, Charles Kenny McClatchy, in 1883 (McQuiston, 1989); Similarly, Frank Gannett, the founder of the Gannett Company in 1923, relinquished a management responsibilities after 32 years in 1955, by which Gannett had become the largest newspaper chain in the U.S. ("The Press," 1957).

Private newspaper owners' motivations in general were to achieve business success but also to have personal influence in the public discourse and affairs of their communities. Research has found private individual newspaper owners trade profit for maximizing personal opinion and social influence by utilizing newspapers as opinion platforms (Meyer, 2009; Picard, 2014), and family-owned media have even more ties to local, social, and political establishments (Powers et al., 2014; Tajpour et al., 2021). In other words, these private owners were often willing to forgo a portion of their profits in order to maximize their influence through their journalism and editorial policies.

There were no particular management conflicts during the private newspaper ownership era because owners usually held the management position as well. Most private newspapers served a single community or city, so organizations during this era were small and simple. For example, prior to the industrial revolution and urbanization of the late nineteenth century, circulations for a single private newspaper usually were less than

1000 and rarely exceeded 2000 (Emery, 1972). This small-scale operational structure allowed private owners to exercise control over the newspaper by either acting as managers or by closely monitoring and directing organizational operations (Demers, 1996; Picard & Van Weezel, 2008). Because private owners participated in the newsroom management, the roles of owners and managers highly overlapped. For example, prior to the industrial revolution and urbanization of the late nineteenth century, circulations for a single private newspaper usually were less than 1000 and rarely exceeded 2000 (Emery, 1972). This small-scale operational structure allowed private owners to exercise control over the newspaper by either acting as managers or by closely monitoring and directing organizational operations (Demers, 1996; Picard & Van Weezel, 2008). So they conveniently sought influence in their communities and had considerable power and influence over the news (Bagdikian, 2004; Picard, 2014). Schwoebel (1976) found that private individual owners operated with "newsroom autonomy," with owners often embedding their personal opinions into the story selection process and the specialization of the topic of the story. Likewise, Breed's study (1955) on social control in the newsroom revealed that private owners possess the formal authority to establish the newspaper's policy, which may shape or influence the news in a particular direction. In Breed's examination of editorial employees in the newsroom, approximately half of participants expressed the need to self-censor in accordance with the predetermined news judgments and editorial content set by the owners (Breed, 1955).

During the mid-twentieth century when broadcast media gained popularity, newspapers experienced a substantial decline in their media market shares as audience and advertisers moved to the airwaves (Rosenstiel, 1990). Radio and television directly affected daily newspapers because these mediums attracted a mass viewing audience, which in turn offered very efficient mediums for national advertisers (Swayne, 1969). For instance, the National Broadcasting Company (NBC), which is the oldest major broadcast network in the U.S., was established by Radio Corporation of America (RCA) in 1926 and focused on a national market rather than solely on local and regional aspects (Campbell et al., 2011). Newspapers also lost the competition to television. For example, daily newspapers were unable to fully capture the dramatic events of

1963 neither when President John F. Kennedy was assassinated nor when the subsequent killing of his accused killer, which unfolded on TV (Andrew, 2019). In other words, newspapers were no longer the audience and advertisers' only choice, and competition escalated from intra-industry to inter-industry.

Overall, the development of the U.S. newspaper industry can be attributed to the contributions of private individuals and rich families since 1704 (Bryan & Merrill, 1993). Private newspaper owners also had made great wealth from this monopoly when they were the only medium in the market (Bass, 1999), and many of them were willing to sacrifice a significant portion of their profit in order to establish social influence and cultivate ties with the political establishments within their community (Schwoebel, 1976). The monopoly held by newspapers was disrupted with the emergence of broadcast media in the mid-twentieth century (Demers, 1996; Picard & Brody, 1997). Radio and TV attracted a larger mass audience through their entertainment programing and captivating performance, consequently undermining newspapers' advertising revenue (Campbell et al., 2011). Moreover, the competitive landscape for newspapers became more challenging, making it increasingly difficult for private newspaper owners to solely manage their operations. The uncertain future led to the potential consolidation of some small- and medium-sized privately owned newspapers with larger corporate newspaper firms (Schwoebel, 1976; Hollifield, 2012).

Public Newspaper Ownership Era (Around 1960s–2010)

The trend toward the concentration of ownership in the newspaper industry began in the early part of the twentieth century, leading to the emergence of corporate newspaper ownership (Demers, 1996). The first newspaper company to go public was Dow Jones (publisher of the *Wall Street Journal*), which joined the NYSE in 1963, followed by Gannett (publisher of *USA Today*), which moved to the NYSE in 1967 (Kirchhoff, 2009).

As time passed, an increasing number of small privately owned newspapers began merging with larger privately owned newspaper firms. For example, the number of newspaper owners reached its historical peak around 1910, with 2153 owners operating 2202 newspapers, but by 1940, the number of owners had declined 25 percent to 1619, while the total number of newspapers remained relatively unchanged (Emery, 1972).

The trend of newspaper ownership concentration, or the selling of businesses by many private newspaper owners, can be attributed to several factors. First, during the 1950s and 1960s, the newspaper industry faced significantly higher expenditures for printing and electronic equipment (Swayne, 1969). This was necessary to compete with radio and television stations, which were increasingly cutting into advertising sales and profits; thus, newspaper owners were confronted with capital demands larger than ever before (Swayne, 1969).

As the newspaper business structure grew more complex and specialized, private family descendants became less knowledgeable about the intricacies of the business or were unable to personally manage all aspects themselves (Underwood, 1995). Consequently, they started relying on professionals in various roles, including journalists, salespeople, and publishing house staff, to handle the day-to-day operations (Gade, 2008; Sylvie & Gade, 2009). Moreover, if some descendants did not have the ability or interest to continue running the newspaper and they planned to sell it, the capital gains taxes that they needed to pay would be a huge financial hit on the family's wealth (Demers, 1996). The capital gains tax rate is the increased value of an asset depending on the profit for the year (Ghaeli, 2016). If considering how profitable the newspaper business was in the mid of twentieth century, this tax on the descendants of private family owners was almost 25 percent in the 1960s (Luscombe, n.d.). Therefore, in order for the family to maintain the wealthy and privileged lifestyles, merging into a large corporate newspaper firm was the descendants' best choice (Demers, 1996; Lacy et al., 1996). For example, Joseph Pulitzer started as a successful newspaper publisher of the *St. Louis Post-Dispatch* (purchased in 1878) and the *New York World* (purchased in 1883), then worked to use the *New York World* to advance his political party's ideas and programs (Gade, 2006). Joseph Pulitzer ultimately rose to prominence as a key national figure within the Democratic Party and founded Pulitzer Prizes in 1917 (Topping, n.d.). However, the following generations in the Pulitzer family were not able to keep their business. Pulitzer III led the company to go public in 1986 (Gade, 2006). For instance, the *St. Louis Post-Dispatch* now is owned by Lee Enterprises (Investors, 2005).

Furthermore, large corporate newspaper owners recognized the potential for significant revenue by allowing individuals to invest in their companies, as they observed the development of the stock market (Hollifield, 2012). The stock market is a marketplace where investors can buy and sell shares or stocks of publicly traded companies (Chen, 2022). After its decades of development since the late 1700s and its recovery in the 1930s from the stock market crash of 1929—a period known as the Great Depression—the U.S. New York Stock Exchange became the world's largest stock exchanges; During World War II—from 1939 until the end of the war in late 1945—the Dow Jones Industrial Average increased by 50 percent (Carlson, 2020). A great number of companies started to join and seek financial support (Hayes, 2022). In other words, the stock market opened the door for the public to invest in newspapers in ways that provided a great potential revenue source and contributed to the U.S. newspaper ownership shifting from the private era to the public era (Hollifield, 2012).

However, the opportunity of the stock market was available to just a few large corporate newspaper firms due to the rigorous listing requirements of the Initial Public Offering (IPO) (Emery, 1972). Filing an IPO is the first step for a company to sell its stock to the public, and meeting the IPO's listing requirements instills confidence in public shareholders that the company is mature enough for future growth (Fernando, 2022). It is a challenge to meet the listing requirements of an IPO. For example, companies filing an IPO in 2023 to join the New York Stock Exchange (NYSE) are required to have aggregate pre-tax earnings of at least $12 million in the previous three years, with a minimum of $5 million in the most recent year (NYSE, n.d.). The first newspaper company to go public was Dow Jones (publisher of the *Wall Street Journal*), which joined NYSE in 1963, and Gannett (publisher of *USA Today*) moved to NYSE in 1967 (Kirchhoff, 2009).

As a result of their public ownership, the level of newspaper profit began to be reported and made public and common stockholders quickly realized that these newspaper companies held considerable value with significant profit margins. For example, on the 1967 Fortune list, the New York Times Company ranked No. 38 with $173 million, while the smallest company in top 500 U.S. public companies was $129 million (Swayne, 1969). Newspaper operating profit margins historically had been in the 10 to 15 percent range, but then ranged between 20 and 30 percent and sometimes even higher in the few publicly traded newspaper companies (Soloski, 2005; also see Picard, 2005). Furthermore, newspapers attracted many institutional investors when they recognized that the newspaper companies' profit margins increased significantly and frequently exceeded Standard and Poor's 500 (S&P 500) (Soloski, 2005; also see Picard, 2005), which was at most 6.5 percent through the 1960s and 1980s (Philosophical Economics, 2014). The S&P 500 is a stock market index that measures the performance of the 500 largest publicly traded companies listed on U.S. exchanges, while it is also commonly used as a benchmark to track and forecast the overall direction of economic performance (Kenton, 2020; Denis et al., 2003). In short, if a stock profit margin is higher than that of the concurrent S&P 500 index, it would show this stock is valuable to purchase or invest in.

The financial support from the stock market prompted the newspaper industry to become a national industry and started a new round of mergers and acquisitions (Demers, 1996; Underwood, 1995). During the 1960s to the 1980s, the substantial wealth generated from selling stock to the public motivated publicly traded newspapers to embark on rapid expansion (Picard & Van Weezel, 2008). For example, between 1960 and 1980, 57 newspaper owners sold their properties to one single owner—Gannett (Demers, 1996). By the late 1990s, public newspaper ownership dominated the newspaper industry with more than half of U.S. newspapers owned by public newspaper corporations (Hollifield, 2012).

Beyond the primary advantage of improving the economic situation, research also indicates that public newspaper firms achieved other positive benefits. For instance, they have developed more specialized coverage areas, as evidenced by studies conducted by Picard and Brody (1997) and Demers (1996). Public newspaper firms have the capacity to cover multiple communities and cities, enabling them to expand their reporting on multicultural society and minority communities, thereby ensuring sensitivity to the needs and wishes of those groups (Demers, 1996; Picard & Brody, 1997). As newspapers sought to diversify their content to cater to a broader range of communities and received sufficient financial support through the stock market, there was a notable increase in the number of reporters and editors, and the newspaper industry as a whole experienced a 40 percent increase in the number of journalists from 1960 to 1980 (Wright & Lavine, 1982). Moreover, the economic stability of public newspaper firms also played a role in increasing journalists' job satisfaction, as noted by Beam (2006).

On the other hand, this transition from privately owned to publicly traded newspaper companies has been a subject of controversy. Many scholars, journalists, and citizens express concerns that economic missions of owners in publicly traded firms may conflict with the principles of democratic journalism (Merrill, 2011; also see Lowrey & Gade, 2011; Lacy et al., 2014). As businesses, newspaper companies must strive to generate profits within the legal framework of the U.S. capitalistic system, but as institutions, newspapers are part of the U.S. press, which carries certain social responsibilities (Swayne, 1969). Particularly, the pressure to maintain a constantly growing stock price became the primary motivation for public newspaper owners, which exacerbated the owners' emphasis on profit margins and forced the journalists to produce more advertising-oriented content, thus deemphasizing the journalists' flexibility and autonomy in making judgments about coverage of news (Soloski, 2005; also see Picard, 2005). Along with the gradual intensification of working with the capital market—with Wall Street analysts and investors—the marketing spirit swept through public newspaper owners' mindsets, which influenced and compromised journalists' and editors' professional perspectives (Underwood, 1995). The newsroom started incorporating marketing concepts into its daily operations, treating news as a product and readers as target audiences. Newspaper editors adopted a mindset focused on satisfying the "audience's taste" and adhering to "market ethics" in their news selection process, so there was a shift toward publishing more lifestyle stories and a reduction in government coverage (Meyer, 2009). In the market-oriented newsroom, owners view readership as a market and news as a product designed to appeal to that market, so editors focus more on satisfying the needs of the audience and advertisers (Lacy & Martin, 2004), rather than prioritizing sufficient coverage for "monitoring" the government's activities (Merrill, 2011; also see Lowery & Gade, 2011). For example, some studies showed that newspapers with strong market orientation might undermine their journalistic obligation in community service (Beam, 2002; Lacy et al., 1996). These operational conflicts developed a new concept—market-driven journalism (McManus, 1997). By definition, this is a type of journalism that pays close attention to readers' wants and needs when making judgment about content (Beam, 2002, 2006), but this "market judging" may harm or replace "journalistic judgement" (McManus, 1997), and leave less coverage of government issues and more coverage about people's "self-fulfillment life" (Underwood, 1995). Moreover, in a team-based newsroom, editors find themselves spending an increasing amount of time facilitating other non-editorial departments, primarily due to growing market pressures (Gade, 2004). In short, news editors have for decades tried to balance the often conflicting needs of a democracy-oriented journalism mission with economic pressures.

However, this balance was disrupted with the advent of the digital age. Starting around 2000, the development of internet-based media became more prominent because of their low-cost news consumption and flexible reading experience (Webster & Ksiazek, 2012). Meanwhile, the rise of 24/7 internet-based media led to an expansion of alternative news sources, which largely eroded the audience's attention, and directly impacted the adverting dollars as advertisers turned away from newspapers and toward digital media (Carpenter & Petersen, 2017; Picard, 2014). Consequently, the credit ratings of newspaper companies within the industry were downgraded (Bary, 2010). Newspaper corporations' falling share prices reflect a lack of shareholder confidence, resulting in more people wanting to sell their stock rather than buy it (Channick, 2021; Boudoukh et al., 2013). With Internet-based media offering readers low-cost and flexible news consumption options, the newspaper industry was forced to consider digital transformation strategies (Picard, 2009; Chyi & Chadha, 2012). This includes evaluating different digital devices and platforms to understand audience preferences and their unique information-processing behaviors (Eveland Jr et al., 2002).

In reality, despite extended effort, public newspaper companies have struggled to replace their traditional business model with new models that can effectively compete in the digital world (Picard, 2010). They transformed their print businesses at an operation level, but did not act to adapt to digital technologies (Hess et al., 2016; Kane et al., 2015). In the early age of internet development around the 1990s, newspapers saw the internet as an efficient way to reach a broader audience and more advertisers, so most newspapers created a free online presence as a complement to their offline sales (Martens et al., 2018; Picard, 2010). However, the online audience does not adhere to the traditional production cycle of daily newspapers, which operates on a 24-hour base, or publishing one print edition per day. In contrast, online media outlets have much shorter new cycles, often lasting less than 45 minutes on average (Cagé et al., 2019). When newspapers tried to adjust to the Internet audience's expectations by providing more free content, the result was less than expected: short production cycles left little time for content quality control, and the news articles in different editions' newspapers began to overlap (Martens et al., 2018). The traditional newspaper audience became less willing to subscribe when the paper content and quality became the same as the free content online (Martens et al., 2018). Some newspapers tried the opposite—using a "paywall" to restrict and protect their high-quality content (Chyi, 2012). The first paywall was implemented in 1997 by the *Wall Street Journal* charging a $50 fee per year. However, some research has found that implementing a paywall is not a good solution because of the ubiquitous presence of alternative online news sources. The paywall actually led to a 51 percent decrease in online visits and thus advertising revenue for the newspaper industry as a whole (Chiou & Tucker, 2013). In short, public newspapers have largely failed in their digital transformational strategies, primarily because the revenue generated from digital sources cannot make up for the revenue they have lost since the decline of the traditional newspaper industry (Picard, 2010; Chyi & Ng, 2020).

While newspapers were already facing revenue challenges due to the rise of new media, the 2008 economic recession exacerbated this situation. Because many businesses had tightened their advertising in response to the recession, public newspapers had to largely cut their operation budget to maintain the appearance of a better profit margin in the stock market (Kirchhoff, 2009). This led to a string of layoffs in the industry. For example, McClatchy announced 1600 layoffs (15 percent of its workforce) in 2009, A.H. Belo (renamed DallasNews) announced 500 cuts and 413 buyouts in 2009, and Gannett offered buyouts and layoffs for up to 1400 employees in 2011–2012 (Sonderman, 2012). Several prominent newspaper chains, including the Tribune Company, the Journal Register Company, and Philadelphia Newspapers LLC, faced financial difficulties and filed for bankruptcy in the aftermath of the 2008 recession (La Merced, 2009).

In sum, the era of public ownership spanned nearly 50 years, from when the *Wall Street Journal* went public in 1963 through the first decade of twenty-first century (Kirchhoff, 2009). During this time, newspapers' above-average profitability immediately attracted the attention of shareholders and investors (Soloski, 2005), and thus huge financial support was infused into the U.S. newspaper industry (Picard & Van Weezel, 2008). From the 1960s to the 1990s, newspapers enjoyed financial support and resources to serve multiple communities and cities (Picard & Brody, 1997) and increase the journalist workforce for the reporting of more coverage areas (Wright & Lavine, 1982). To maintain a continually growing share price, public newspaper owners eventually started a wave of intense mergers and cost control, but the public ownership period was still characterized by increasing market orientation and greater awareness of profit expectations in newsrooms (Demers, 1996; Underwood, 1995). However, newspapers' digital transformational strategies failed after a decade of trial and error (Martens et al., 2018). Not only did they lose the audience and advertisers (Chiou & Tucker, 2013), but they also greatly dampened stock market confidence for their future development. Thus, public newspapers relied on aggressive cost control strategies for better performance in profit margin in order to try to restore Wall Street's confidence (Kirchhoff, 2009).

Hedge Fund Newspaper Ownership Era (Around 2010 to Present)

Because of public newspapers' poor business situations, shareholders and common investors have lost confidence in their future. For example, from 2008 to 2022, the combined circulation of print and digital editions of U.S. newspapers decreased by 51 percent, from 49.1 million to 24.3 million., and advertising revenue dropped 74.1 percent from $37.8 billion to $9.8 billion (Pew Research Center, 2023). Moreover, the market size of the U.S. newspaper was valued at $18.39 billion in 2022, and it is expected to continually decrease 6.5 percent in the next eight years (Grand View Research, n.d.). These numbers have been reflected in newspaper companies' share price. For instance, Gannett's share price sharply decreased from $24.19 per share in 2015 to $1.95 per share in 2024 (Gannett/Historic Share Prices, n.d.). Dallas News Corporation's share price decreased from $69.32 in 2008 to $3.78 per share in 2024 (NASDAQ: DALN, n.d.).

However, public newspaper companies' low share price is not reflective of the value of their tangible resources. These companies own properties across the country, which hedge funds are highly interested in (Morgenson & Rosner, 2023; Lo, 2001). The first documented acquisition of a publicly owned newspaper occurred in 2010 when Alden Global Capital acquired Digital First Media (DFM), one of the largest national newspaper chains with 56 daily newspapers in 12 states, including *Denver Post* (Sydney, 2018). This acquisition was made through DFM's parent company, MediaNews Group, and was valued at $1 billion at the time. However, the deal was not entirely in cash, it also included the debt the company assumed Chasan, 2010). However, the trend of newspaper ownership shifting to ownership by hedge funds has gained more attention in the academic world following Alden's completion of its acquisition of Tribune Publishing in 2021. At the time, Tribune was the nation's third largest newspaper publisher and known for its flagship paper *Chicago Tribune* (Channick, 2021; Coppins, 2021). By 2021, more and more of the largest daily newspaper companies were acquired by hedge funds (Maher, 2021), bringing the newspaper industry into the era of hedge fund ownership.

A hedge fund is a type of private equity firm, but it has a very different motivation and approach to investment decisions, especially compared with most common equity firms (Stulz, 2007). Common private equity firms tend to invest in long-term strategies and seek to invest in companies that are stable, well managed and have potential to grow (Meyer, 2009). These include firms such as Fidelity, which is known as the first retirement plan provider (Chen, 2024). Long-term investment private equity firms usually need to hold an interest in an acquisition for three to five years but more often for seven to ten years. Although their eventual goal is to maximize profit return, they seek to improve the company through management changes, streamlining operations, or expansion (Wright et al., 2009). Most equity firms do not seek governance control, and do not pressure companies' boards of investors for faster expansion and aggressive cost control (Szajowski & Łebek, 2007). In contrast, hedge funds are short-term investment private equity firms and tend to target public companies with poor economic situations (Achleitner & Kaserer, 2005). Hedge funds tend to use leverage, or borrowed money, and other risky financial practices to increase their returns (Lo, 2001). Because hedge funds focus on short-term investment and borrow substantial debt and loans, promising investors high returns, they need to convert company assets into cash to repay their investors and provide the high returns they expect (Stulz, 2007). Therefore, under hedge fund ownership, there are few assets left for the development of the companies they acquire to operate, resulting in limited sustainable long-term prospects (Morgenson & Rosner, 2023).

Moreover, the most apparent difference with common equity firms is that hedge funds treat company ownership or full governance control as a necessary objective for maximum profit return (Kahan & Rock, 2017). In short, newspapers have accepted private equity firms, also referred to as institutional investors, as common financial tools (Picard, 1994), but see hedge funds as threats due to their harvesting motivation.

In the newspaper industry, only a few hedge funds have been targeting newspaper companies, but their impact has been significant. Alden Global Capital, founded in 2007, is the most active one (Edmonds,

2011). Alden first attracted public attention in 2010, and has accelerated its interest in the newspaper industry. For example, in 2019, Alden attempted a hostile takeover of Gannett in the stock market. At the time, Gannett was the largest newspaper chain in the U.S. with 261 daily newspapers, including *USA Today, Detroit Free Press, Daily News Journal,* in 48 states (Gannett Annual Report, 2019). Although Gannett successfully prevented this attack (O'Connell & Brown, 2019), Tribune Publishing (the publisher of *Chicago Tribune* and *Los Angeles Times*) was not so lucky. As Alden's next target, Tribune Publishing was successfully acquired in 2021 (Coppins, 2021). As the third largest newspaper publisher in the U.S., Tribune Publishing once owned 11 daily newspapers, including *Chicago Tribune* and *Los Angeles Times* (Alpert, 2021). Alden later attempted to acquire Lee Enterprises (owning 77 daily newspapers in 26 states) but was rejected in 2021 (Mullin, 2021). To date, Alden is collectively the second-largest owner of newspapers in the U.S. with more than 200 daily newspapers (Coppins, 2021). In addition, McClatchy, another well-known national newspaper chain in 29 U.S. markets with 30 newspapers, including *Minneapolis Star-Tribune, The Miami Herald,* and *The Kansas City Star,* was acquired by another hedge fund—Chatham Asset Management—in 2020 (Hall, 2020). Chatham was founded in 2003, a bit earlier than Alden, but this hedge fund does not concentrate on the U.S. newspaper business only. It has expanded into Canada: In 2016, Chatham took over Canada's largest newspaper chain, Postmedia, which owned more than 100 newspapers in Canada (Lee, 2020).

Newspaper companies face a big challenge with hedge fund ownership's aggressive concentration on profit return, and this can be seen in the process of hedge funds' action plans. Broadly speaking, hedge funds tend to aim for undervalued companies with "cheap" stock prices and sufficient tangible assets that can be replaced with immediate profit return (Brav et al., 2015; Coppins, 2021). In order to achieve this goal, hedge funds assume governance control or company ownership to quickly gut tangible assets and save the cost of their investment (Coppins, 2021; Kahan & Rock, 2017).

In addition, hedge funds tend to aim for well-developed industries because they usually have considerable tangible assets, and if these assets combined with low stock price, they would be attractive for hedge funds to target (French, 2022; Phan, 2021). In the newspaper industry, tangible assets include real estate, printing plants, distribution networks, people, etc. (Massey, 2016).

Moreover, industry-wide characteristics serve as analysis benchmarks or indicators, so hedge funds can minimize the investment cost (Wong, 2020). With this analysis process of hedge funds, public newspaper companies are the perfect acquisition targets. Newspaper companies' falling stock prices means they are "cheap" (Ghaeli, 2016), but the term "cheap" stock may have a deeper meaning to investors: undervalued. Undervalued is a financial term that refers to a situation where a company's stock price is below its true intrinsic value (Dittmar & Field, 2016). The stock price normally reflects shareholder confidence in the company's future development (Szajowski & Łebek, 2007), while the intrinsic value of the company is the present value of all tangible assets (Dittmar & Field, 2016). In addition, there is a widely used financial tool by which investors evaluate whether a certain company is "cheap" or considered undervalued—the price-to-earnings ratio (P/E), which is derived from the company's price per share and earnings per share (Ghaeli, 2016). Price per share indicates the market price of a stock, while earnings per share determine the profit that can be shared to each common stock (Arsal, 2021). In other words, undervalued companies are those with low P/E ratios, which reflect the shareholder's scarce confidence about the companies' future economic growth (Szajowski & Łebek, 2007). The large public newspaper firms that have been targeted have failed to compete in the digital age, so they don't have enough profit return—low earnings per share—and not many shareholders are interested in their stocks—low price per share. However, if a company does not generate any profit for the past year, it simply won't have an available P/E ratio value (Ghaeli, 2016). For example, Tribune Publishing had different negative free cash flow amounts: in 2017 (-$8.7 billion), in 2018 (-$54 billion), and in 2019 (-$39.2 billion) (Tribune Publishing Annual Reports, 2017, 2018, 2019), but this wasn't reflected with different P/E ratios. Instead, all showed the P/E ratios were not available (Yahoo Finance, n.d.). In addition, P/E ratio can be used to compare a company's own historical record or to compare it to the average niche market value (Ghaeli, 2016). In short, the lower the P/E ratio, the "cheaper" or more undervalued the company.

Other financial factors that hedge funds typically use to determine target companies include free cash flow and tangible assets (Stulz, 2007). Free cash flow refers to the cash remaining after a company has covered its operating expenses and capital expenditures, representing its profit (Bhandari & Adams, 2017). In terms of sufficient tangible assets, as a well-developed industry (Stulz, 2007), newspapers usually have plenty of physical newsrooms and buildings, where hedge funds can get a predictable amount of return at the time of selling (Barnier, 2021). Ultimately, hedge funds choose when to take actions to acquire companies. They attempt to take advantage of opportunities created by significant transactional events, such as spin-offs, mergers and acquisitions, reorganizations, bankruptcies, and other extraordinary corporate transactions (Stulz, 2007). For example, Chatham Asset Management hedge fund acquired McClatchy right after this newspaper company filed for bankruptcy in 2020 (Hall, 2020). Alden Global Capital pursued Tribune Publishing when their board chair—Michael, Ferro—sold his 25% stake in the company to Alden at the time he left the board position in 2019 (Davidow, 2020).

Aggressive corporate control is also inevitable for hedge funds when they acquire companies due to their short lock-up period, which refers to a specific timeframe during which investors are restricted from redeeming their investment from the hedge funds (Garbaravicius & Dierick, 2005). Hedge funds usually operate by borrowing money from other institutional investors (i.e., banks and insurance companies) to invest or buy targeted public firms (Amaded, 2021). In previous studies, hedge funds, as a type of private equity firm, have also been considered institutional investors (Brav et al., 2015). Hedge funds get this money at low interest rates because the loans are short-term (an average of nine months to a year) (Achleitner & Kaserer, 2005). To control the risks of repaying the loans, hedge funds make money by quickly selling off the companies' assets (Ghaeli, 2016; Stulz, 2007). This short-term sell-off strategy aims for immediate profit return. It also gives hedge funds time to use these profits as equity to borrow more money to purchase more companies through leveraged buyouts (Ghaeli, 2016). The lock-up period reflects the idea that the hedge fund will pay high dividends as long as one waits to redeem their investment until after the hedge fund has had time to sell off the assets from its leveraged buyouts (Achleitner & Kaserer, 2005). In contrast, normal equity firms also operate their business with a lock-up policy, but it is usually extended to around five or ten years (Achleitner & Kaserer, 2005), so the corresponding strategies are less aggressive. In short, hedge funds try to avoid any long-term strategies, seeing them as investment costs to avoid; therefore, it becomes necessary to take full ownership of newspaper companies they acquired. Accordingly, this action has been called a harvesting strategy, a metaphor for a take-the-money-and-run strategy (Meyer, 2009).

Particularly in the newspaper industry, the academic study of the effects of hedge fund ownership is new, but many existing practical cases illustrate hedge funds' harvesting strategy in the newspaper industry. Hedge funds pose many existential challenges to the U.S. newspaper industry, such as gutting the newsrooms and laying off a great number of editorial employees just after new owners assume control (Coppins, 2021). For example, two days after the acquisition of Tribune Publishing was finalized, Alden Global announced an aggressive round of buyouts that let go at least 10 percent of the newsroom workforce (Edmonds, 2020); in another month, it sold *Chicago Tribune*'s valuable century-old headquarters in downtown and moved the paper's headquarters to a smaller, less centrally located, and inexpensive building in a remote suburb (Coppins, 2021). Tribune Tower was a high-rise building that (with the Sears Tower) was a definitive element of downtown Chicago's skyline. To sell the tower was a visible sign of the paper's demise as a Chicago institution. While Alden was gutting the workforce and the buildings of the *Chicago Tribune*, its Manhattan-based owners had never physically visited the paper (Coppins, 2021).

When hedge funds' aggressive harvesting actions in the company they own increase, the operational conflicts also increase (Stulz, 2007). For example, a recent survey study uses the phrase "the wolf at the door" to describe the impact of hedge fund activism on corporate governance, and the results show that behind the door is severe cost control in long-term investment on targeted firms, particularly a reduction in research and development (Coffee Jr & Palia, 2016). In addition, when private equity groups such as hedge funds acquire a publicly traded company, the change in ownership makes the company private (Bharath & Dittmar,

2010). Leaving the stock market allows the hedge fund to target the company's cash flow. That cash flow is used pay off debts they borrowed from other investments including banks to make the acquisition in the first place (Bharath & Dittmar, 2010; Macey et al., 2008). Meanwhile, by going private without the stock market and public supervision, hedge funds have no responsibility to report the amount of money they are making to the public and even to the investors they borrowed the money from; hedge funds can also implement a rigid corporate governance and gut an industry quickly and efficiently (Brav et al., 2015; Kahan & Rock, 2017; Stulz, 2007). In fact, a hedge fund-owned company going private is a regular phenomenon in some businesses (Stulz, 2007), but in the news industry, which claims a democratic mission and First Amendment freedoms, having owners govern a company with only a desire to sell off assets for profit is a major social problem (Meyer, 2009).

Moreover, ownership-management conflicts become more challenging because hedge fund owners only value tangible assets and have a different perspective base of management. Journalism professional values refer to newspapers' social responsibilities (Bryan & Merrill, 1993), and editors/journalists are educated and trained to work for community service (Christians et al., 2010). These all have been regarded as important intangible assets by the previous newspaper owners, and they are immediately abandoned by hedge fund owners. Additionally, in the academic field of hedge fund management, agency theory is widely applied (Buchanan et al., 2014) and assumes that owners must monitor and control agents (managers) to safeguard the owners' residual claims from the potential self-interest and actions of the agents (Bansal, 2013). Through the lens of agency theory, journalism professionalism is a kind of self-interest because serving the public does not meet the owner's requirement of profit (Buchanan et al., 2014).

Overall, hedge funds' ownership motives are drastically different from public newspaper ownership in the news industry, as they focus solely on short-term profit, whereas publicly held companies prioritize both profit and long-term company development (Coppins, 2021). For hedge funds, assuming ownership to harvest the company, rather than develop it, is the easier and faster way to produce profit. Its short lock-up period helps hedge funds borrow a large amount of money from banks and other institutional investors with low-interest loans, but this also forces them to sell off the assets of the company even more quickly and aggressively (Achleitner & Kaserer, 2005). Therefore, hedge fund ownership poses an existential challenge to the U.S. newspaper industry in meeting its democratic mission, and it creates a substantial conflict between owners and news staff whose values are journalistic.

Summary

There are three newspaper ownership eras throughout the development of the U.S. newspaper industry, starting with private newspapers, expanding in the nation with public newspapers, then facing great threats with hedge fund ownership. Beginning in 1704, private newspapers were owned by individuals and then their rich families. The growth of the industry and urban population increased the size and wealth of newspapers, but it also accelerated the competitive environment within the newspaper industry in the twentieth century. The competition included increasing challenges from broadcast media (Bagdikian, 2004; Bass, 1999), the need for capital to update and modernize existing printing presses and facilities (Swayne, 1969), and changing tax structures (Fernando, 2022). These challenges eventually led many private owners to give up their heritage of passing on ownership from one generation to the next, and by the 1960s, were instead selling their newspapers (Meyer, 2009).

Hence, some major newspaper corporations or chains developed through mergers and acquisitions with small newspapers in the twentieth century (Demers, 1996). Entering the stock market accelerated the growth of public newspaper ownership with the financial support from investors (Hollifield, 2012). Public newspaper ownership became prevalent since the 1960s (Picard & Van Weezel, 2008). However, when entering the digital age around 2000, the newspaper industry couldn't compete with digital media in all three markets—audience, advertiser, capital, which all changed their interests to social or search media (Albarran, 2016), so many major public companies' stock prices fell and companies even fell into bankruptcy. At last, hedge funds arrived with lots of money for acquiring newspapers but they are not heroes: They are harvesters squeezing the last drop of profit (Coppins, 2021).

In terms of the roles of management in the U.S. newspaper industry, the idea of dual missions—making money as business yet striving for quality journalism—has always existed in all three eras of ownerships. In the private (family) newspaper ownership era, editorial control was with the publisher, who often was hands-on with management (Schwoebel, 1976), and ownership was motivated by political and social influence, as well as wealth, and at times accepted lower profits to maintain their influence and prestige (Picard, 2014). In public newspaper ownership era, newspapers developed a more complex organizational structure, and they were managed by professional managers, whose work was reflection of their expertise and professional values (Soloski, 2005; also see Picard, 2005). Public newspapers sought to attract investors by maintaining high profits (Demers, 1996), but the perception was that quality journalism produced sufficient profits (Galbraith, 2015). However, in the hedge fund ownership era, most newsrooms remain managed by professional journalists, yet hedge funds seek to control these journalism managers by selling off the firms' tangible assets and reducing staff and resources for quality journalism (Bryan & Merrill, 1993; Coppins, 2021).

References

Achleitner, A. K., & Kaserer, C. (2005). *Private equity funds and hedge funds: A primer* (No. 2005-03). Working Paper.
Albarran, A. B. (2016). *The media economy*. Routledge.
Albarran, A. B., Mierzejewska, B., & Jung, J. (Eds.). (2018). *Handbook of media management and economics*. Routledge.
Alpert, L. (2021, April). Alden Clashes with billionaire over future of Tribune – And of local news. *The Wall Street Journal*. https://www.wsj.com/articles/alden-clashes-with-billionaire-over-future-of-tribuneand-of-local-news-11618027398?mod=hp_lead_pos7
Amaded, K. (2021, November). Who invests in hedge funds – And why? *The Balance*. https://www.thebalance.com/who-invests-in-hedge-funds-and-why-3306239

Andrew, L. (2019, July). 50 ways the news industry has changed in the last 50 years. *Stacker.* https://stacker.com/stories/3312/50-ways-news-industry-has-changed-last-50-years

Arsal, M. (2021). Impact of earnings per share and dividend per share on firm value. *ATESTASI: Jurnal Ilmiah Akuntansi, 4*(1), 11–18.

Bagdikian, B. H. (2004). *The new media monopoly: A completely revised and updated edition with seven new chapters.* Beacon Press.

Bansal, P. (2013). Inducing frame-breaking insights through qualitative research. *Corporate Governance: An International Review, 21*(2), 127–130.

Barnier, B. (2021). Hedge fund. *Investopedia.* https://www.investopedia.com/terms/h/hedgefund.asp

Bary, A. (2010). Today's news: Washington Post is dirt cheap. *Barron's.* https://www.barrons.com/articles/SB125477134071631

Bass, J. (1999). Newspaper monopoly. *American Journalism Review, 21*(6), 64–64.

Beam, R. A. (2002). Size of corporate parent drives market orientation. *Newspaper Research Journal, 23*(2-3), 46–63.

Beam, R. A. (2006). Organizational goals and priorities and the job satisfaction of US. Journalists. *Journalism & Mass Communication Quarterly, 83*(1), 169–185.

Bhandari, S. B., & Adams, M. T. (2017). On the definition, measurement, and use of the free cash flow concept in financial reporting and analysis: A review and recommendations. *Journal of Accounting and Finance, 17*(1), 11–19.

Bharath, S. T., & Dittmar, A. K. (2010). Why do firms use private equity to opt out of public markets? *The Review of Financial Studies, 23*(5), 1771–1818.

Boudoukh, J., Feldman, R., Kogan, S., & Richardson, M. (2013). *Which news moves stock prices? A textual analysis* (No. w18725). National Bureau of Economic Research.

Brav, A., Jiang, W., & Kim, H. (2015). Recent advances in research on hedge fund activism: Value creation and identification. *Annual Review of Financial Economics, 7*, 579–595.

Breed, W. (1955). Social control in the newsroom: A functional analysis. *Social Forces*, 326–335.

Bryan, C. R., & Merrill, J. C. (1993). *The dialectic in journalism: Toward a responsible use of press freedom.* LSU Press.

Buchanan, J., Chai, D. H., & Deakin, S. (2014). Agency theory in practice: A qualitative study of hedge fund activism in Japan. *Corporate Governance: An International Review, 22*(4), 296–311.

Cagé, J., Hervé, N., & Viaud, M. L. (2019). The production of information in an online world: Is copy right?. Available at SSRN 2672050.

Campbell, R., Martin, C. R., & Fabos, B. (2011). *Media and culture: An introduction to mass communication.* Macmillan.

Carlson, B. (2020, January). The relationship between war & the stock market. *A Wealth of Common Sense.* https://awealthofcommonsense.com/2020/01/the-relationship-between-war-the-stock-market/

Carpenter, R. E., & Petersen, B. C. (2017). Capital market imperfections, high-tech investment and new equity financing. *Finance Markets, the New Economy and Growth*, 143–170.

Channick, R. (2021, May). Tribune Publishing offering buyouts to newsroom employees, two days after purchase by hedge fund Alden. *Chicago Tribune.* https://www.chicagotribune.com/business/ct-biz-tribune-publishing-newsroom-buyouts-alden-20210526-ihthwykitjfmrpnj63whhlqw5i-story.html

Chasan, E. (2010, January). MediaNews owner files prepackaged bankruptcy. *Reuters.* https://www.reuters.com/article/lifestyle/medianews-owner-files-prepackaged-bankruptcy-idUSTRE60M019/

Chen, J. (2022, July). What is the stock market? *Investopedia.* https://www.investopedia.com/terms/s/stockmarket.asp

Chen, J. (2024). Private equity explained with examples and ways to invest. *Investopedia.* Retrieved from https://www.investopedia.com/terms/p/privateequity.asp

Chiou, L., & Tucker, C. (2013). Paywalls and the demand for news. *Information Economics and Policy, 25*(2), 61–69.

Christians, C. G., Glasser, T., McQuail, D., Nordenstreng, K., & White, R. A. (2010). *Normative theories of the media: Journalism in democratic societies.* University of Illinois Press.

Chyi, H. I. (2012). Paying for what? How much? And why (not)? Predictors of paying intent for multiplatform newspapers. *International Journal on Media Management, 14*(3), 227–250.

Chyi, H. I., & Chadha, M. (2012). News on new devices: Is multi-platform news consumption a reality? *Journalism Practice, 6*(4), 431–449.

Chyi, H. I., & Ng, Y. M. M. (2020). Still unwilling to pay: An empirical analysis of 50 US newspapers' digital subscription results. *Digital Journalism, 8*(4), 526–547.

Coffee, J. C., Jr., & Palia, D. (2016). The wolf at the door: The impact of hedge fund activism on corporate governance. *Annals of Corporate Governance, 1*(1), 1–94.

Coppins, M. (2021, October). A secretive hedge fund is gutting newsrooms. *The Atlantic.* https://www.theatlantic.com/magazine/archive/2021/11/alden-global-capital-killing-americas-newspapers/620171/

Davidow, S. (2020, May). The state of journalism at Tribune Publishing. *The NewsGuild.* https://newsguild.org/the-state-of-journalism-tribune-publishing/

Demers, D. (1996). Corporate newspaper structure, editorial page vigor, and social change. *Journalism & Mass Communication Quarterly, 73*(4), 857–877.

Denis, D. K., McConnell, J. J., Ovtchinnikov, A. V., & Yu, Y. (2003). S&P 500 index additions and earnings expectations. *The Journal of Finance, 58*(5), 1821–1840.

Dittmar, A., & Field, L. C. (2016). Do corporate managers know when their shares are undervalued? New evidence based on actual (and not just announced) stock buybacks. *Journal of Applied Corporate Finance, 28*(4), 73–85.

Edmonds, R. (2011, July). Who is investor Randall Smith and why is he buying up newspaper companies? *Poynter.* https://www.poynter.org/reporting-editing/2011/randall-smith-alden-global-capital-newspaper-companies/

Edmonds, R. (2020, July). Alden buyouts have eliminated more than 10% of Tribune Publishing newsroom staffing in just six weeks. *Pointer.* Retrieved from https://www.poynter.org/locally/2021/alden-buyouts-have-eliminatedmore-than-10-of-tribune-publishing-newsroom-staffing-in-just-six-weeks/

Emery, E. (1972). *The press and America: An interpretative history of the mass media.* Prentice-Hall.

Eveland, W. P., Jr., Seo, M., & Marton, K. (2002). Learning from the news in campaign 2000: An experimental comparison of TV news, newspapers, and online news. *Media Psychology, 4*(4), 353–378.

Fernando, J. (2022, June). What is an Initial Public Offering (IPO)? *Investopedia.* https://www.investopedia.com/terms/i/ipo.asp

French, D. (2022, May). Hedge fund Elliott chases oil and gas deals, bucking Wall Street. *Reuters.* https://www.reuters.com/markets/us/hedge-fund-elliott-chases-oil-gas-deals-bucking-wall-street-2022-05-25/

Gade, P. (2006). No ordinary Joe: A life of Joseph Pulitzer III. *Journalism History, 32*(2), 118.

Gade, P. J. (2004). Newspapers and organizational development: Management and journalist perceptions of newsroom cultural change. *Journalism & Communication Monographs, 6*(1), 3–55.

Gade, P. J. (2008). Journalism guardians in a time of great change: Newspaper editors' perceived influence in integrated news organizations. *Journalism & Mass Communication Quarterly, 85*(2), 371–392.

Galbraith, J. K. (2015). *The new industrial state*. Princeton University Press.

Gannett/Historic Share Prices. (n.d.). Gannett Co., Inc. (GCI) Stock Historical Prices & Data. *Yahoo Finance*. Retrieved from https://finance.yahoo.com/quote/GCI/history/

Garbaravicius, T., & Dierick, F. (2005). Hedge funds and their implications for financial stability. *ECB Occasional Paper* (34).

Ghaeli, M. R. (2016). Price-to-earnings ratio: A state-of-art review. *Accounting, 3*(2), 131–136.

Grand View Research. (n.d.). U.S. newspaper market size, share & trends analysis report by type (digital, print), by revenue generation (circulation, advertising, others), by region, and segment forecasts, 2022–2030. https://www.grandviewresearch.com/industry-analysis/us-newspaper-market

Hall, K. (2020, August). Bankruptcy judge approves the sale of McClatchy to hedge fund Chatham Asset Management. *McClatchy*. https://www.mcclatchydc.com/news/nation-world/national/article244710217.html

Hayes, A. (2022, April). How does the stock market work? *Investopedia*. https://www.investopedia.com/articles/investing/082614/how-stock-market-works.asp

Hess, T., Matt, C., Benlian, A., & Wiesböck, F. (2016). Options for formulating a digital transformation strategy. *MIS Quarterly Executive, 15*(2).

Hollifield, A. (2012). Changing perceptions of organizations. *Changing the news: The forces shaping journalism in uncertain times*, pp. 193–212.

Investors. (2005, January). *Pulitzer Chooses Lee Enterprises to Continue Its Newspaper Legacy*. Retrieved from https://investors.lee.net/news-releases/news-release-details/pulitzer-chooses-lee-enterprises-continue-itsnewspaper-legacy

Kahan, M., & Rock, E. B. (2017). Hedge funds in corporate governance and corporate control. In *Corporate Governance* (pp. 389–461). Gower.

Kane, G. C., Palmer, D., Phillips, A. N., Kiron, D., & Buckley, N. (2015). Strategy, not technology, drives digital transformation. *MIT Sloan Management Review and Deloitte University Press, 14*(1–25).

Kenton, W. (2020, March). 10-K. *Investopedia*. Retrieved from https://www.investopedia.com/terms/1/10-k.asp

Kirchhoff, S. M. (2009). *US newspaper industry in transition* (Vol. 40700). Congressional Research Service.

Kovach, B., & Rosenstiel, T. (2021). *The elements of journalism, revised and updated 4th edition: What newspeople should know and the public should expect.* Crown Publishing Group.

La Merced, M. (2009, September). Freedom communications files for bankruptcy protection. *The New York Times.* https://www.nytimes.com/2009/09/02/business/media/02freedom.html

Lacy, S., & Martin, H. J. (2004). Competition, circulation and advertising. *Newspaper Research Journal, 25*(1), 18–39.

Lacy, S., Shaver, M. A., & Cyr, C. S. (1996). The effects of public ownership and newspaper competition on the financial performance of newspaper corporations: A replication and extension. *Journalism & Mass Communication Quarterly, 73*(2), 332–341.

Lacy, S., Stamm, M., & Martin, H. (2014). Short-run decisions threaten papers' long-run viability. *Newspaper Research Journal, 35*(4), 6–20.

Lee, E. (2020, July). Under hedge fund set to own McClatchy, Canadian newspapers endured big cuts. *The New York Times.* https://www.nytimes.com/2020/07/16/business/media/hedge-fund-chatham-mcclatchy-postmedia-newspapers.html

Lo, A. W. (2001). Risk management for hedge funds: Introduction and overview. *Financial Analysts Journal, 57*(6), 16–33.

Lowrey, W., & Gade, P. (2011). *Changing the news.* Routledge.

Lowrey, W., & Gade, P. J. (2012). Connective journalism. In *Changing the news* (pp. 270–286). Routledge.

Luscombe, M. (n.d.). Historical capital gains rates. Wolters Kluwer. https://www.wolterskluwer.com/en/expert-insights/whole-ball-of-tax-historical-capital-gains-rates

Macdonald, I. (2006). Teaching journalists to save the profession: A critical assessment of recent debates on the future of US and Canadian journalism education. *Journalism Studies, 7*(5), 745–764.

Macey, J., O'Hara, M., & Pompilio, D. (2008). Down and out in the stock market: The law and economics of the delisting process. *The Journal of Law and Economics, 51*(4), 683–713.

Maher, S. (2021, December). What does hedge fund ownership mean for local news outlets? *Marketplace.* https://www.marketplace.org/2021/12/02/what-does-hedge-fund-ownership-mean-for-local-news-outlets/

Martens, B., Aguiar, L., Gomez-Herrera, E., & Mueller-Langer, F. (2018). The digital transformation of news media and the rise of disinformation and fake news.

Massey, B. L. (2016). Resource-based analysis of the survival of independent web-native news ventures. *Journalism & Mass Communication Quarterly, 93*(4), 770–788.

McManus, J. H. (1997). Who's responsible for journalism? *Journal of Mass Media Ethics, 12*(1), 5–17.

McQuiston, J. T. (1989, April). Charles K. McClatchy, 62, dies; led newspaper company in west. *The New York Times*. https://www.nytimes.com/1989/04/17/obituaries/charles-k-mcclatchy-62-dies-led-newspaper-company-in-west.html

Merrill, J. (2011). Journalism and democracy. *Changing the news: The forces shaping journalism in uncertain times*, pp. 45–62.

Meyer, P. (2009). *The vanishing newspaper: Saving journalism in the information age*. University of Missouri Press.

Morgenson, G., & Rosner, J. (2023). *These are the plunderers: How private equity runs – And Wrecks – America*. Simon and Schuster.

Mullin, B. (2021, November). Lee enterprises enacts poison pill to guard against Alden takeover. *The Wall Street Journal*. https://www.wsj.com/articles/lee-enterprises-enacts-poison-pill-to-guard-against-alden-takeover-11637793121

NASDAQ: DALN (n.d.). DallasNews Corporation Series A Common Stock (DALN). *Nasdaq*. Retrieved from https://www.nasdaq.com/market-activity/stocks/daln

NYSE. (n.d.). Overview of NYSE quantitative initial listing standards. *NYSE*. Retrieved from https://www.nyse.com/publicdocs/nyse/listing/NYSE_Initial_Listing_Standards_Summary.pdf

O'Connell, J., & Brown, E. (2019, February). A hedge fund's 'mercenary' strategy: Buy newspapers, slash jobs, sell the buildings. *The Washington Post*. https://www.washingtonpost.com/business/economy/a-hedge-funds-mercenary-strategy-buy-newspapers-slash-jobs-sell-the-buildings/2019/02/11/f2c0c78a-1f59-11e9-8e21-59a09ff1e2a1_story.html

Pew Research Center. (2023, November). Newspapers Fact Sheet. https://www.pewresearch.org/journalism/fact-sheet/newspapers/

Phan, T. T. (2021). A former hedge fund trader founded America's leading non-alcoholic craft beer. *Hustle*. https://thehustle.co/01202021-athletic-brewery-nonalcoholic/

Philosophical Economics. (2014, March). Profit margins: The death of a chart. Retrieved from https://www.philosophicaleconomics.com/2014/03/foreignpm/

Picard, R. G. (1994). Institutional ownership of publicly traded US newspaper companies. *Journal of Media Economics, 7*(4), 49–64.
Picard, R. G. (2005). Unique characteristics and business dynamics of media products. *Journal of Media Business Studies, 2*(2), 61–69.
Picard, R. G. (2009). Why journalists deserve low pay. *The Christian Science Monitor, 19*(9).
Picard, R. G. (2010). The future of the news industry. *Media and Society, 5,* 365–379.
Picard, R. G. (2014). Twilight or new dawn of journalism? Evidence from the changing news ecosystem. *Journalism Practice, 8*(5), 488–498.
Picard, R. G., & Brody, J. H. (1997). *The newspaper publishing industry.* Allyn and Bacon.
Picard, R. G., & Van Weezel, A. (2008). Capital and control: Consequences of different forms of newspaper ownership. *The International Journal on Media Management, 10*(1), 22–31.
Powers, A., Broadrick Sohn, A., & Briggs-Bunting, J. (2014). Family-owned newspapers: Filling niches in local US communities. *Journal of Media Business Studies, 11*(2), 79–91.
Rosenstiel, T. B. (1990, April). As the nation's publishers meet in Century City, they face severe troubles on advertising and circulation fronts. *Los Angeles Times.* https://www.latimes.com/archives/la-xpm-1990-04-23-fi-76-story.html
Schwoebel, J. (1976). *Newsroom democracy: The case for independence of the press.* na.
Shoemaker, P. J., & Reese, S. D. (2013). *Mediating the message in the 21st century: A media sociology perspective.* Routledge.
Soloski, J. (2005). Taking stock redux: Corporate ownership and journalism of publicly traded newspaper companies. *Corporate Governance of Media Companies,* 59–76.
Sonderman, J. (2012, June). 600 newspaper layoffs in one day is, unfortunately, not a record. *Poynter.* https://www.poynter.org/reporting-editing/2012/600-newspaper-layoffs-in-one-day-is-unfortunately-not-a-record/
Stulz, R. M. (2007). Hedge funds: Past, present, and future. *Journal of Economic Perspectives, 21*(2), 175–194.
Swayne, E. E. (1969). *The last families: A study of metropolitan newspaper ownership, 1950–1967.* Northwestern University.
Sydney, E. (2018, April). Denver post rebels against its hedge-fund ownership. *The New York Times.* https://www.nytimes.com/2018/04/07/business/media/denver-post-opinion-owner.html

Sylvie, G., & Gade, P. (2009). Changes in news work: Implications for newsroom managers. *Journal of Media Business Studies, 6*(1), 113–148.
Szajowski, K., & Łebek, D. (2007). Optimal strategies in high risk investments. *Bulletin of the Belgian Mathematical Society-Simon Stevin, 14*(1), 143–155.
Tajpour, M., Salamzadeh, A., Salamzadeh, Y., & Braga, V. (2021). Investigating social capital, trust and commitment in family business: Case of media firms. *Journal of Family Business Management.*
The Press: The Chain That Isn't. (1957, December). *Time.* http://content.time.com/time/subscriber/article/0,33009,893804,00.html
Topping, S. (n.d.). Biography of Joseph Pulitzer. *Pulitzer. Org.* https://www.pulitzer.org/page/biography-joseph-pulitzer
Underwood, D. (1995). *When MBAs rule the newsroom.* Columbia University Press.
Webster, J. G., & Ksiazek, T. B. (2012). The dynamics of audience fragmentation: Public attention in an age of digital media. *Journal of Communication, 62*(1), 39–56.
Wong, Y. T. F. (2020). Wolves at the door: A closer look at hedge fund activism. *Management Science, 66*(6), 2347–2371.
Wright, B. E., & Lavine, J. M. (1982). *The constant dollar newspaper: An economic analysis covering the last two decades.* Inland Daily Press Association.
Wright, M., Amess, K., Weir, C., & Girma, S. (2009). Private equity and corporate governance: Retrospect and prospect. *Corporate Governance: An International Review, 17*(3), 353–375.
Yahoo Finance. (n.d.). Retrieved from https://finance.yahoo.com/quote/GCI/

3

Journalism Professionalism's New Struggles

Abstract This chapter will review the development of journalism norms in a democratic society, focusing on how social responsibility theory evolved from libertarian theory and how journalism professionalism has been established and developed in the U.S. It will also examine the conflicts between journalism professional norms and the advent of digital technology, as well as the industry's uncertain competitive landscape.

Keywords Journalism professional value • Social responsibility theory • Journalism norms • Digital media technology • Newspaper industry

The role of journalism norms in society has been widely studied since World War II (Merrill, 1974; Siebert et al., 1956). Particularly in a democratic society, the press as an independent of government institution is charged with telling citizens the truth so they can function as informed citizens (Siebert et al., 1956). In tension with these normative functions, economic stress or financial pressure have been discussed as factors working against journalism quality in the study of the U.S. journalism industry (Lacy & Martin, 1998), due to the conflicts with capitalism in a democratic society (Streeck, 2011). Economic independence can support press freedom (Merrill, 1974), but an overbearing demand on profit margin might hurt journalism quality by squeezing the tangible resources (Lacy & Martin, 1998), such as the number of journalists and physical newsrooms (Usher, 2015). When journalism quality cannot be maintained, publicly held newspaper companies might lose their economic value and thus become vulnerable in the stock market and powerless against hedge funds' attacks as they come to harvest the remaining assets (Coppins, 2021).

Normative theory explains the role of journalism norms in a society. It describes the way that a media system is controlled and influenced by the social system (Merrill, 1974, 1989). The two most widely used theories that relate to the role of journalism in a democratic society are libertarian theory and social responsibility theory (Siebert et al., 1956). The libertarian theory was developed to protect freedom of the press from authoritarian governments, while the social responsibility theory evolved from libertarian theory after WWII when faith in human rationality waned in the wake of the war and its many atrocities (Siebert et al., 1963). This evolution suggests that a free press is obliged to be responsible to society or the public interest with a higher standard (Merrill, 1974, 1989; Siebert et al., 1963). Social responsibility theory has dominated the media system in the U.S. since the mid-twentieth century (Merrill, 1974; Siebert et al., 1956). In terms of libertarian theory, freedom of press is a natural right that reflects people's individual perspectives, but social responsibility theory emphasizes public welfare, so freedom of speech should adhere to shared value standards of accuracy, minimizing harm, and accountability.

Newspapers gradually lost their market share in audience and advertising markets as digital media began to rapidly grow and the internet emerged in the media industry landscape in the early twenty-first century. This created serious economic pressure in the capital markets (Picard, 2009). Sustainable financial support is not only crucial for maintaining journalism autonomy and independence from government influence, but also facilitates the development and corporate expansion of newspapers (Demers, 1996; Merrill, 1974). However, since most newspaper companies are publicly owned and listed in the stock market (Demers, 1996), and because Wall Street does not tolerate stock price and profit margin downturns (Meyer, 2009), newspaper companies face increasingly tougher economic pressures. These pressures have resulted in aggressive cost control measures to improve profit margin performance, including employee layoffs and reduced future investments, both of which undermine newspapers' long-term sustainability (Albarran et al., 2018).

Hedge fund ownership is worthy of study because it represents an extension of the negative effects that profit-driven activities can have on the newspaper industry. As active equity institutions, hedge funds prioritize immediate profit return from publicly traded companies and often disregard intangible values within a company or industry (Fernando, 2021; Morgenson & Rosner, 2023; Stulz, 2007). As for the newspaper industry, journalism norms are a typical intangible resource (Massey, 2016). Therefore, exploring the main challenges to journalism quality and professionalism under hedge fund ownership is important. The newspaper industry played a crucial role in establishing and developing journalism norms, with print journalists being major contributors to journalism professional values in the U.S. (Siebert et al., 1956). Understanding how journalism norms were established and developed within the U.S. newspaper industry might explain the potential consequences of hedge fund newspaper ownership. For hedge funds, the newspaper industry is an attractive and profitable business to harvest (Coppins, 2021), but for a democratic society, a decline and even disappearance of the newspaper industry would jeopardize freedom of expression (Siebert et al., 1956).

The Role of Journalism in a Democratic Society

In terms of normative theory, the purposes of journalism are best understood in relation to the claims made about a good society and what the press should do to facilitate it (Siebert et al., 1956). Normative theories of journalism provide reasoned explanations for the selection of media content, aiming to help the public address and solve societal problems (Christians et al., 2009). As the media system has grown since World War II, there has been a need to define and articulate the roles and functions of the mass media in society; different media systems reflect the characteristics of the social systems from which they have emerged and developed (Christians et al., 2009).

The development of the democratic social system and the role of journalism took place over centuries, beginning in sixteenth-century England when people resisted regulations imposed by authority figures, such as churches and governments (Siebert et al., 1956). Also as an Anglo-American concept, libertarian theory originated in the seventeenth- and eighteenth-century Europe (Siebert et al., 1956). Libertarian thinkers upheld the belief that freedom of expression is an inherent right of humans (Siebert et al., 1956; Merrill, 1974), and viewed government as the primary obstacle to liberty (Siebert et al., 1956). Consequently, libertarians argued that the press should be free from the government control in order to serve as a safeguard against governmental encroachments on individual liberty, enlightening the public and protecting the rights of individuals (Siebert et al., 1956). A democratic society is founded on principles of respecting individual freedom, equal rights, and a tolerance for knowledge and truth (Merrill, 1974, 1989). During the early stages of the development of the democratic social system, characterized by the underlying libertarian theory, the press fought for freedom of expression and was marked by partisanship and lack of restraint (Siebert et al., 1956). Siebert further observes that this partisanship diminished in the nineteenth century and the early twentieth century with the emergence of objective journalism (Siebert et al., 1956). Objective journalism sought to distinguish factual reporting from opinion columns, and the dissemination of "facts of the day" became a primary responsibility of journalists (Siebert et al., 1956, p. 61).

However, as the democratic social system became more complex in the twentieth century, there was a growing skepticism regarding the inherent ability of humans to naturally discern truth from falsehood solely based on their rationality. For instance, the twentieth century saw two world wars in the first 45 years, with World War II alone resulting in the deaths of nearly 70–85 million people worldwide (O'Neill, 2024). These events made people doubt whether those in powerful positions could end the world, prompting the need for more responsible press. The shift in thinking from libertarian theory to social responsibility theory was driven by these concerns (Siebert et al., 1963). Siebert and Peterson also noted (1963) that the twentieth century witnessed technological and industrial revolutions, leading to the expansion of media size and publishing efficiency, while urbanization was accompanied by a growing volume of advertising and larger audiences. In this changing landscape, with technological advancements and increased competition (Merrill, 1974), fewer media companies possessed the capability to effectively serve diverse communities with a single daily newspaper, thereby potentially leading to the domination of media by a few socioeconomic groups (Siebert et al., 1963). Consequently, the freedom of the press was threatened, including issues concerning the accessibility of mass communication and the representativeness of minority communities (Pickard, 2014).

Social responsibility theory, building upon libertarian theory, brought about a redefinition of traditional press functions (Siebert et al., 1963). Libertarians viewed humans as rational beings capable of making decisions and driven to seek truth, seeing them as fundamental units of civilization (Siebert et al., 1956). In contrast, advocates of social responsibility theory believed that individuals have a civic duty and should act in ways that benefit society as a whole; meanwhile, they argued that media should prioritize promoting democratic processes and enlightening the public, rather than solely focusing on their own economic interests or providing entertainment (Siebert et al., 1963). In essence, the development of social responsibility theory represented a shift from the emphasis on negative freedom in libertarian theory to positive freedom associated with ethics and responsibility. More precisely, while libertarian theory contended that removing most restrictions on the press would allow the truth to emerge, social responsibility theory recognized that negative freedom alone was insufficient (Siebert et al., 1963). Instead, it argued that effective freedom should encompass freedom of the press for "achieving the goals defined by its ethical sense and by society's needs" (Siebert et al., 1963).

The intellectual climate of the twentieth century favored the development of social responsibility theory. This climate encompassed a collective mentality that emerged from dominant thought patterns in areas such as ethics, religion, and science, which were prevalent among educated individuals (Siebert et al., 1963). These thought patterns or worldviews were influenced by broader intellectual developments, including Darwinian evolution and modern physics. These concepts challenged the Enlightenment's belief in unchanging laws of nature and aligned with a more collectivist perspective on society, which formed the philosophical basis of social responsibility theory (Siebert et al., 1963). Furthermore, the emergence of new media platforms in the twentieth century necessitated a foundation of journalism knowledge to support journalists in providing "variety, quantity and quality information" to the educated public (Siebert et al., 1963). In short, as the media landscape expanded, there was a growing recognition of the importance of journalistic expertise and the need to uphold certain standards in the profession.

In sum, in terms of libertarian theory, the primary role of journalism in a democratic society is to inform and serve the needs of individuals (Merrill, 1974, 1989), but social responsibility generally replaced libertarian theory in the mid-twentieth century (Siebert et al., 1963). This shift occurred as the social system became more complex, new technologies developed, and criticism increased from an educated public (Merrill, 1974; Siebert et al., 1956). Libertarian theory was developed to resist government control and focused on people's natural right to free expression (Siebert et al., 1956). Social responsibility theory, on the other hand, emerged primarily due to a shift in the intellectual climate, recognizing that free journalism was in danger, particularly in terms of the limited accessibilities for minority communities (Siebert et al., 1963). The journalism profession's spirit emerged in response to the growing demand for journalism knowledge and moral values, emphasizing the sense of public welfare (Siebert et al., 1963).

Journalism Professionalism

As stated by sociologists, a profession is characterized by the adoption of a shared values among its participants (Abbott, 1988; Goode, 1957). It assumes that participants can be trusted due to their expertise, which distinguishes them from laypeople (Merrill, 1974; Beam, 1990). Different studies have identified various key attributes of professions. Becker and Vlad conducted a comprehensive review (2011) and found that the most frequently mentioned characteristics include specialized knowledge, working autonomy, a focus on public service over economic gain, shared values with institutions, education, the production of unstandardized product, and the expectation of a lifelong occupation. Additionally, some scholars have emphasized the importance of licensing (Barber, 1963; Becker & Vlad, 2011), which is commonly accepted in many professional domains but not in the field of journalism.

Several scholars argue that journalism, unlike medicine and law, is not a full profession and is instead considered a semi-profession (Tumber & Prentoulis, 2005; McQuail, 2000; Shoemaker & Reese, 1996). Discussions about journalism as a profession have been ongoing since the early twentieth century, coinciding with the emergence of the concept of journalism's professional spirit (Weaver et al., 2009; Merrill, 1974). There are concerns that the traditional characteristics of a profession may be too restrictive for journalism, as journalists require a certain degree of freedom to assess news value (Merrill, 1974). This is one reason why journalists have not historically been required to obtain professional licenses (Merrill, 1974). However, journalism does possess other professional characteristics, such as shared values and ethical codes (Merrill, 1974; Beam et al., 2009).

The earliest of ethical codes, known as the Canons of Journalism, was adopted by the American Society of Newspaper Editors in 1923 (Siebert et al., 1963; Merrill, 1974). This code emphasized the importance of newspapers practicing responsibility toward "the general welfare, sincerity, truthfulness, impartiality, fair play, decency, and respect for the individual's privacy" (Siebert et al., 1963). It also called for press to promote democratic government by facilitating the self-correcting process (Siebert et al., 1963). Furthermore, the development of public newspaper ownership in twentieth century played a role in supporting the formation of ethical codes, as a growing number of journalists belonged to organizations or homogeneous groups that developed similar values (Merrill, 1974).

These ethical codes were developed by experienced journalists and, in conjunction with the growing professional spirit, were likely fostered in part by journalism schools (Merrill, 1974). In the nineteenth century, much of the news was distorted, biased, or used as a political weapon (Siebert et al., 1963). However, this situation began to change when journalism schools emerged in the early twentieth century. These journalism schools not only taught journalism techniques such as writing and editing, but also increasingly emphasized the responsibilities of the media

(Siebert et al., 1963). As college education was recognized as the primary means of developing expertise in the field, journalism schools and departments saw significant growth in the twentieth century (Becker & Vlad, 2011; also see Lowrey & Gade, 2012). Obtaining a degree in journalism and mass communication became the most common qualification for becoming a professional journalist (Weaver et al., 2009; Wilensky, 1964; also see Zelizer, 2004). As the number of students pursuing journalism increased, news organizations began to attract and recruit more individuals with a college degree in journalism (Siebert et al., 1963). These educated individuals set high standards and formulated codes of ethics for their work as journalists (Weaver et al., 2009).

In the digital age, the high professional standards of journalism have weakened and diminished due to shifts of its authority and influence within the news and information industry (Lacy et al., 2014). This loss of professional standards has emerged as result of the idea that everyone is a publisher and can do the work of journalists simply by making ideas and events public (putting them online or in social media). The growth in "citizen journalism" reflects this idea, which has been facilitated by technological convergence. Citizens are not only sources of information or the audience, but also recorders and creators of news (Mythen, 2010). Furthermore, the demand for profit margins from newspaper owners, driven by the stock market, has led to a shift in focus toward profit and business success. Consequently, there is less attention paid to journalism quality, resulting in a reduction of journalism's influence among the public (Lacy & Rosenstiel, 2015).

The advent of the Internet and subsequent digital products has presented traditional newspaper companies with two unprecedented challenges. First, many new digital media platforms are now able to provide the same value that were once exclusive to traditional media, such as accessing news sources, determining the significance of information, and effectively conveying news (Picard, 2009). These alternative media platforms have not only attracted audiences, but also caused advertisers to divert a significant portion of their advertising budget away from traditional newspapers and toward these digital media platforms (Chyi, 2012). Second, in an attempt to counter this economic disadvantage, newspaper owners have increasingly promoted and invested in their own digital media products, while paying more attention to market-driven journalism, treating the audience as customers and prioritizing entertainment-oriented stories over hard news (McManus, 1994; Preston, 2009; Underwood, 1995). These actions, including shorter publication processes and reduced coverage of hard news, have negatively impacted the prestige of newspapers in the field of journalism, making them even more vulnerable in the stock market (Chyi, 2012; Lacy & Sohn, 2011).

The advent of the Internet has disrupted the traditional newsroom landscape by allowing numerous digital news outlets to enter the information market (Lacy & Sohn, 2011). The abundance of digital media has provided a much wider range of news sources, diminishing the audience size of traditional newspapers and their authoritative position as primary news providers (Picard, 2009). This has also challenged traditional journalism values regarding the ability to access sources or analyze data (Picard, 2009). In response to the competition from digital media, the newspaper industry began embracing certain ideas, such as the belief that "online content must be free" (Carlson, 2003, p. 54) and the notion that "it is impossible to charge for general news content" (Herbert & Thurman, 2007, p. 215; also see Chyi, 2012). For example, a national survey of 767 U.S. online adults regarding their news consumption behavior revealed that while there was a strong willingness to pay for newspapers in print format, the same newspapers' online formats (Web & apps) experienced weak paying intent due to the availability of numerous alternative and free online news sources (Chyi, 2012). Furthermore, although the paying intent remains stronger for print versions, it has been unable to counteract the significant decline in daily newspaper circulation. According to a U.S. census survey, the total weekday circulation of U.S. daily newspapers was 55.8 million in 2000 but had dropped to 24.2 million by 2020 (Grundy, 2022). Moreover, many legacy news organizations began promoting various digital products (Beam & Meeks, 2012), resulting in the adoption of a 24/7 news cycle as the norm in newsrooms. This, in turn, led to a decline in the value placed on accuracy (Chyi, 2012).

Furthermore, the market logic of treating audiences and advertisers as "customers" (McManus, 1994; Underwood, 1995) has gradually permeated newsrooms. In order to cater to these "customers," news organizations often prioritize the production of entertainment-oriented content in response to market conditions (McManus, 1994). This prioritization of profits over a secondary concern for journalism leads to a decline in the quality of journalism (Lacy & Sohn, 2011).

Additionally, as discussed in the previous chapter, public newspaper ownership dominated U.S. newspaper companies from the 1960s through the rest of twentieth century, and these owners were primarily driven by their companies' financial performance in the stock market (Demers, 1996). With the emergence of numerous digital media platforms leading to a decline in overall company revenue (Chyi, 2012), owners sought to maintain profit margins as a key performance indicator, making aggressive cost control the primary organizational goal for public newspaper owners (Pristin, 2013). Consequently, rounds of layoffs and the selling off physical newsrooms have had a detrimental impact on journalism quality and the adherence to professional norms within (Coppins, 2021).

In conclusion, the spirit of journalism professionalism emerged early in the twentieth century and was codified after World War II with the development of social responsibility theory (Siebert et al., 1963). Journalism is considered a semi-profession as it requires more freedom compared to traditional professions (Merrill, 1974; Weaver et al., 2009). While traditional professions typically require a legal license, journalism places greater importance on college education and training (Siebert et al., 1963; Merrill, 1974), which fosters the development of high moral and ethical standards in journalism (Becker & Vlad, 2011). However, these high standards have been challenged due to the advancements in digital technology and changes in people's news consumption behaviors (Picard, 2009). In short, balancing economic pressures and maintaining journalism quality has become a challenging task for newspaper owners, particularly as economic pressures have become more persistent (Lacy & Martin, 2004; Lacy & Sohn, 2011).

Hedge Fund Ownership's Influence

Hedge funds, like typical financial institutions, pay close attention to the profit return organizational strategy when acquiring a business (Morgenson & Rosner, 2023; Stulz, 2007). When a hedge fund takes ownership of a newspaper company, it immediately shifts the entire organizational goal toward extracting money from tangible assets, with no interest in intangible resources (Coppins, 2021; Morgenson & Rosner, 2023; Stulz, 2007). For example, an aggressive buyout plan was announced just a week after Tribune Publishing was acquired by a hedge fund (Coppins, 2021). This buyout plan mainly impacted Tribune Publishing's newsrooms, which had garnered 28 Pulitzer Prizes since 1987 (Chicago Tribune Staff, 2022). The Pulitzer Prize is the most prestigious award recognizing achievements in multiple categories of journalism within the United States (Pulitzer.org, n.d.).

While a profit-oriented strategy is not inherently wrong, if it becomes imbalanced and neglects the concerns of journalism quality, it conflicts with the missions of newspapers to uncover truths, foster a marketplace of ideas, and serve broader societal and democratic goals (Lowrey & Gade, 2012, p. 63). For example, a profit-oriented approach may lead to aggressive cost control, undermining the newsrooms' ability to serve the public (Beam & Meeks, 2012). In particular, having fewer journalists on staff with heavier workloads and a greater focus on entertainment coverage has been viewed as eroding journalism professionalism and quality (Beam & Meeks, 2012). Moreover, aggressive cost control efforts often result in newspapers relocating their physical workplaces from downtown headquarters to smaller or suburban districts (Usher, 2015). This relocation effort was aimed at increasing short-term revenue to appease the stock market (Pristin, 2013). Human resources and newsroom physical locations challenge professionalism because of their scarcity (Massey, 2016).

During the period of public newspaper ownership, maintaining this balance had become difficult, leading several newspaper companies such as McClatchy in 2020 (Hall, 2020) and Tribune Publishing from 2008 to 2013 (Baker & Pandey, 2012) to file for bankruptcy. This challenging situation worsened under hedge fund ownership. According to the NewsGuild labor union at Digital First Media—a media company fully controlled by Alden Global hedge fund—the number of journalists at all acquired newspapers rapidly declined after hedge funds assumed ownership (DeCosta-Kilpa, 2018). For example, two daily newspapers in Pennsylvania—*The Pottstown Mercury* and *The Norristown Times-Herald*—lost 74 percent of their journalists between 2012 and 2017. *The Denver Post* experienced a 62 percent decline in its journalists workforce between 2012 and 2018, while *St. Paul Pioneer Press* in Minnesota reduced its number of journalists by 84 percent from 2010 to 2020 (DeCosta-Kilpa, 2018).

Moreover, Alden's profit-oriented approach extended to its dealings with physical newsrooms and was characterized by aggression. After acquiring Tribune Publishing, Alden immediately put at least 10 percent of the newsroom's real estate properties on the market for lease or for sale, including its downtown Chicago headquarters (Ori, 2021). In fact, Alden subsidiary Digital First Media is known for its focus on reducing human resources, while its subsidiary Twenty Lake Holdings specializes in optimizing profits from newspaper real estate by selling its property (O'Connell & Brown, 2019).

In sum, hedge fund ownership can hasten the erosion of financial profit and journalism quality, thereby accelerating the decline of public newspaper companies' sustainability and survival (Coppins, 2021). This phenomenon is evident through the implementation of aggressive cost control measures that primarily affect two significant tangible resources: the number of journalists and the companies' real estate properties (DeCosta-Kilpa, 2018; O'Connell & Brown, 2019).

Summary

Freedom of expression and the promotion of a democratic society are the fundamental purposes of journalism in the Anglo-American context (Siebert et al., 1956). However, dominant press theories have evolved and shifted in response to societal developments. The libertarian theory emerged when people were enlightened against authority control, such as that imposed by the church and government, and the concept of free speech gained widespread acceptance as a natural human right (Siebert et al., 1956). However, as technology rapidly advanced and society grew more complex, the freedom of expression came under threat, leading some scholars to argue that the press must consider public welfare more comprehensively (Siebert et al., 1963; Merrill, 1974). Consequently, the social responsibility theory emerged in the mid-twentieth century, built upon the foundational philosophy that the freedom of the press should serve the public welfare and be maintained by individuals with high journalistic ethical standards (Siebert et al., 1963).

Meanwhile, the intellectual climate underwent a transformation due to the increased levels of education among the audience, as well as the development of a professional spirit within journalism schools (Siebert et al., 1963). Professional journalists have received education and training in universities and are guided by professional organizations (Abbott, 1988) that embody the norms of the profession. They self-restrict their behavior, guided by shared values commonly referred to as journalism professional values (Siebert et al., 1963; Merrill, 1974).

This situation underwent a significant change in the twenty-first century as media owners increasingly prioritized heavy economic pressure and profit-oriented goals. Consequently, journalism professionalism declined, and newspapers became more vulnerable (Beam & Meeks, 2012). This shift was primarily triggered by the development of digital technology (Picard, 2009). This shift was primarily triggered by the development of digital technology (Picard, 2009). In the digital age, there is now an information glut—where everyone is a publisher and nearly all information is available for free (Singer, 2012). The need to compete in this digital marketplace has made news industries more market-oriented. Another relevant idea is that because the audience now lives in the digital space, and everyone can publish—citizen journalism (Mythen, 2010)—news media find themselves paying more attention to what people are saying online than going out in their communities to find news. Thus, more and more news is about what people are saying on social media, which—because it exists for free on social media—has no inherent value for the news media firm (Chyi & Yang, 2009). However, the reality demonstrated that newspapers continued to lose their audience and advertiser markets (Chyi, 2012). Furthermore, the newspaper companies' poor performance in their digital transformation strategies further undermined investors' confidence in the stock market (Lacy & Sohn, 2011).

This loss of confidence in the newspaper industry attracted the attention of hedge funds. As purely financial institutions, hedge funds are solely focused on tangible resources and immediate profit return (Stulz, 2007), with no regard for journalism professional norms or intangible resources (Coppins, 2021).

In the upcoming chapter, the direct effects on news managers when a pure financial institution becomes the new owner of their companies will be discussed. When hedge funds as new owners fail to recognize journalism professional values and prioritize profit return above all else, the question arises of how journalism quality can be maintained or how it can continue to support a healthy democratic society.

References

Abbott, A. (1988). *The system of professions: An essay on the division of expert labor.* University of Chicago press.

Albarran, A. B., Mierzejewska, B., & Jung, J. (Eds.). (2018). *Handbook of media management and economics.* Routledge.

Baker, L. B., & Pandey, A. (2012). Publisher Tribune emerges from four-year bankruptcy. *Reuters.* Retrieved from: https://www.reuters.com/article/business/publisher-tribune-emerges-from-four-year-bankruptcy-idUSBRE8BU022/

Barber, B. (1963). Some problems in the sociology of the professions. *Daedalus,* 669–688.

Beam, R. A. (1990). Journalism professionalism as an organizational-level concept. *Journalism and Communication Monographs,* 121.

Beam, R. A., & Meeks, L. (2012). "So Many Stories, So Little Time": Economics, Technology, and the Changing Professional Environment for News Work. In *Changing the News* (pp. 230–248). Routledge.

Becker, L. B., & Vlad, T. (2011). Where professionalism begins. *Changing the news: The forces shaping journalism in uncertain times,* pp. 249–269.

Carlson, D. (2003). The history of online journalism. *Digital Journalism: Emerging Media and the Changing Horizons of Journalism,* 31–56.

Chicago Tribune Staff. (2022, May). Chicago Tribune's 28 Pulitzer Prizes: A list of all the winners. *Chicago Tribune.* https://www.chicagotribune.com/about/ct-chicago-tribune-pulitzer-prizes-20220509-dlxp3pd5hnb5jfomh5z5bxx7wi-story.html

Christians, C. G., Glasser, T., McQuail, D., Nordenstreng, K., & White, R. A. (2009). *Normative theories of the media: Journalism in democratic societies.* University of Illinois Press.

Chyi, H. I. (2012). Paying for what? How much? And why (not)? Predictors of paying intent for multiplatform newspapers. *International Journal on Media Management, 14*(3), 227–250.

Chyi, H. I., & Yang, M. J. (2009). Is online news an inferior good? Examining the economic nature of online news among users. *Journalism & Mass Communication Quarterly, 86*(3), 594–612.

Coppins, M. (2021, October). A secretive hedge fund is is gutting newsrooms. *The Atlantic.* https://www.theatlantic.com/magazine/archive/2021/11/alden-global-capital-killing-americas-newspapers/620171/

DeCosta-Kilpa. (2018). *Inside the 'dehumanizing' cost-cutting efforts by new ownership at the Boston Herald.* Boston.com. Retrieved from: https://www.boston.com/news/media/2018/05/15/boston-herald-digital-first-media/

Demers, D. (1996). Corporate newspaper structure, editorial page vigor, and social change. *Journalism & Mass Communication Quarterly, 73*(4), 857–877.

Fernando, J. (2021, November). Price-to-Earnings (P/E) ratio. *Investopedia.* https://www.investopedia.com/terms/p/price-earningsratio.asp

Goode, W. J. (1957). Community within a community: The professions. *American Sociological Review, 22*(2), 194–200.

Grundy, A. (2022). Service annual survey shows continuing decline in print publishing revenue. *Census.gov.* https://www.census.gov/library/stories/2022/06/internet-crushes-traditional-media.html

Hall, K. (2020, August). Bankruptcy judge approves the sale of McClatchy to hedge fund Chatham Asset Management. *McClatchy.* https://www.mcclatchydc.com/news/nation-world/national/article244710217.html

Herbert, J., & Thurman, N. (2007). Paid content strategies for news websites: An empirical study of British newspapers' online business models. *Journalism Practice, 1*(2), 208–226.

Lacy, S., & Martin, H. J. (1998). Profits up, circulation down for Thomson papers in 80s. *Newspaper Research Journal, 19*(3), 63–76.

Lacy, S., & Martin, H. J. (2004). Competition, circulation and advertising. *Newspaper Research Journal, 25*(1), 18–39.

Lacy, S., & Rosenstiel, T. (2015). *Defining and measuring quality journalism*. Rutgers School of Communication and Information.

Lacy, S., & Sohn, A. B. (2011). Market journalism. *Changing the news: The forces shaping journalism in uncertain times*, pp. 159–176.

Lacy, S., Stamm, M., & Martin, H. (2014). Short-run decisions threaten papers' long-run viability. *Newspaper Research Journal, 35*(4), 6–20.

Lowrey, W., & Gade, P. J. (2012). *Changing the news*. Routledge.

Massey, B. L. (2016). Resource-based analysis of the survival of independent web-native news ventures. *Journalism & Mass Communication Quarterly, 93*(4), 770–788.

McManus, J. H. (1994). *Market-driven journalism: Let the citizen beware?* Sage Publications.

McQuail, D. (2000). Some reflections on the western bias of media theory. *Asian Journal of Communication, 10*(2), 1–13.

Merrill, J. C. (1974). *The imperative of freedom: A philosophy of journalistic autonomy*. Hastings House.

Merrill, J. C. (1989). *The dialectic in journalism*. Uluç, G.

Meyer, P. (2009). *The vanishing newspaper: Saving journalism in the information age*. University of Missouri Press.

Morgenson, G., & Rosner, J. (2023). *These are the plunderers: How private equity runs – And Wrecks – America*. Simon and Schuster.

Mythen, G. (2010). Reframing risk? Citizen journalism and the transformation of news. *Journal of Risk Research, 13*(1), 45–58.

O'Connell, J., & Brown, E. (February, 2019). *A hedge fund's 'mercenary' strategy: Buy newspapers, slash jobs, sell the buildings*. The Washington Post. Retrieved from: https://www.washingtonpost.com/business/economy/a-hedgefunds-mercenary-strategy-buy-newspapers-slash-jobs-sell-the-buildings/2019/02/11/f2c0c78a-1f59-11e9-8e21-59a09ff1e2a1_story.html

O'Neill, A. (2024, February). Estimated number of military and civilian fatalities due to the Second World War per country or region between 1939 and 1945. *Statista*. https://www.statista.com/statistics/1293510/second-world-war-fatalities-per-country/

Ori, R. (2021, January). Chicago Tribune to exit Prudential Plaza, move newsroom to printing facility. *Chicago Tribune*. https://www.chicagotribune.com/business/ct-biz-chicago-tribune-newsroom-prudential-center-20210111-jqeeknsta5e25i22mbmimccwwm-story.html

Picard, R. G. (2009, May). Why journalists deserve low pay. *The Christian Science Monitor*. https://www.csmonitor.com/Commentary/Opinion/2009/0519/p09s02-coop.html

Pickard, V. (2014). *America's battle for media democracy: The triumph of corporate libertarianism and the future of media reform.* Cambridge University Press.

Preston, P. (2009). *Making the news. Journalism and news cultures in Europe.* Routledge.

Pristin, T. (2013, October). Struggling newspapers sell off old headquarters. *The New York Times.* https://www.nytimes.com/2013/10/23/realestate/commercial/struggling-newspapers-sell-off-old-headquarters.html

Pulitzer.org. (n.d.). *The Pulitzer Prizes.* Retrieved from: https://www.pulitzer.org/

Shoemaker, P. J., & Reese, S. D. (1996). *Mediating the message* (pp. 781–795). Longman.

Siebert, F., Peterson, T., Peterson, T. B., & Schramm, W. (1956). *Four theories of the press: The authoritarian, libertarian, social responsibility, and Soviet communist concepts of what the press should be and do* (Vol. 10). University of Illinois Press.

Siebert, F., Peterson, T., & Schramm, W. (1963). *Four theories of the press: The authoritarian, libertarian, social responsibility, and Soviet communist concepts of what the press should be and do.* University of Illinois Press.

Singer, J. B. (2012). Journalism and digital technologies. In *Changing the News* (pp. 213–229). Routledge.

Streeck, W. (2011). The crises of democratic capitalism. *New Left Review, 71,* 5–29.

Stulz, R. M. (2007). Hedge funds: Past, present, and future. *Journal of Economic Perspectives, 21*(2), 175–194.

Tumber, H., & Prentoulis, M. (2005). Journalism and the making of a profession. *Making Journalists: Diverse Models, Global Issues, 58,* 73.

Underwood, D. (1995). *When MBAs rule the newsroom.* Columbia University Press.

Usher, N. (2015). Newsroom moves and the newspaper crisis evaluated: Space, place, and cultural meaning. *Media, Culture & Society, 37*(7), 1005–1021.

Weaver, D. H., Beam, R. A., Brownlee, B. J., Voakes, P. S., & Wilhoit, G. C. (2009). *The American journalist in the 21st century: US news people at the dawn of a new millennium.* Routledge.

Wilensky, H. L. (1964). The professionalization of everyone? *American Journal of Sociology, 70*(2), 137–158.

Zelizer, B. (2004). *Taking journalism seriously: News and the academy / Barbie Zelizer.* Sage. Print.

4

Threats to News Management in the Era of Hedge Fund Ownership

Abstract This chapter will explore the main threats that hedge fund ownership may pose to media management in the newspaper industry. The core assumption is that when the motivation of newspaper owners shifts from prioritizing journalism quality to profit-driven objectives, the role of media management needs to be redefined, and management conflicts increase beyond those that already existed during public ownership.

Keywords Journalism professional value • Media social impacts • Public interests • Newsroom operational objectives • Media management

This chapter will explore the main threats that hedge fund ownership may pose to media management in the newspaper industry. The core assumption is that when the motivation of newspaper owners shifts from prioritizing journalism quality to profit-driven objectives, the role of media management needs to be redefined, and management conflicts increase beyond those that already existed during public ownership. Particularly, by focusing on short-term profit-driven goals, hedge fund ownership may result in a more aggressive reduction of experienced staff and the selling off of essential physical property, without considering the long-term development and potential harm to the social impact of the acquired companies (Morgenson & Rosner, 2023).

Prior to the emergence of hedge fund ownership, during the era of public ownership, several challenges already existed. These challenges included limited resources, such as downsized newsrooms and a decrease in experienced journalists (Whitney et al., 2021), as well as overwhelming job tasks resulting from the digital production realm (Reinardy, 2011, 2012; Picard, 2016). As discussed in the previous chapter, these challenges primarily stem from the broken traditional business model without a clear substitute digital model (Picard, 2011) and the increasing competition from alternative media platforms due to technological advancements (Chyi & Tenenboim, 2019; Lacy et al., 1996). Hedge fund ownership does not provide a solution to these challenges; instead, it adds further complexity to the existing ones due to its primary motivation of immediate profit returns (Channick, 2021; Coppins, 2021).

The role of management became increasingly important in the post-World War II era when some businesses transitioned into knowledge-based industries, and the role of management extends far beyond being a mere extension of ownership (Drucker, 2008). As business enterprises grew in size, their complexity also increased (Stacey, 1995). Consequently, specialized knowledge became a critical asset, giving rise to a new class of individuals known as knowledge workers, who often faced challenges in being integrated into organizations (Drucker, 2008). Therefore, managing knowledge workers posed unique challenges compared to managing unskilled laborers. Managers had to establish objectives aligned with the organization's overall mission and foster shared values that could effectively motivate and engage knowledge workers with diverse educational backgrounds (Dembek et al., 2016; Drucker, 2008). Additionally, recognizing the importance of maintaining a positive social impact became essential for organizations in order to foster loyalty among employees and strengthen their overall position in society (Drucker, 2008; Lindgreen & Swaen, 2010).

Moreover, as described in Chap. 2, it is evident that different types of newspaper ownership have different motivations, and these motivations have shaped the evolution of management practices throughout the various eras of newspaper ownership (Picard & Van Weezel, 2008). The changing ownership motivations pose a challenge for managers, as they constantly struggle to adjust their objectives in order to lead rank-and-file journalists toward meeting the organizational goals predefined by owners (Drucker, 2008). Sylvie and Gade (2009) examined this idea in the newspaper industry, exploring how the balance of managing journalists and meeting owners' goals has been impacted by the uncertainty in the news environment during the first decade of the twenty-first century. Specifically, in recent decades, media managers' objectives often involve adapting to publishing across various media platforms and handling the demands of a sizable staff shortage, along with the challenge of layoffs of experienced staff (Sylvie & Gade, 2009). Consequently, the layoffs of experienced journalists make it more challenging for the media to train younger peers (Blatchford, 2021) and ensure adequate media coverage.

When transitioning into the era of hedge fund ownership, these management challenges may worsen. This can be attributed to the fact that hedge fund ownership does not value quality journalism and fails to provide sufficient organizational resources to the news managers (Coppins, 2021), who not only identify themselves as journalists but also hold management positions (Gade, 2004). As discussed in the previous chapter, hedge funds are primarily concerned with the economic issues and financial value of the businesses they acquire, often leading to a reduction in assets that are hard to measure in monetary terms (Coppins, 2021;Morgenson & Rosner, 2023 ; Stulz, 2007), such as journalism professionalism, public interest, and social responsibilities. Management needs to work with the organizational resources provided by ownership (Drucker, 2008), including both tangible and intangible resources. However, hedge funds often prioritize selling the company's tangible assets and do not value the intangible assets associated with the professional values (Morgenson & Rosner, 2023; Stulz, 2007), such as journalism professionalism (Coppins, 2021). Once they have exploited the company they acquire, they will sell it for whatever profit remains, disregarding any long-term considerations (Morgenson & Rosner, 2023).

Management

The study of management has a long and rich history, which has often been accompanied by an exploration of changing goals and motivations of ownership, as well as organizational structures that are driven by owners' objectives (Gedajlovic & Shapiro, 1998). Specifically, it is important for management to align with the values and motivations of the owners, which should then be congruent with the goals and values of the rank-and-file employees (Drucker, 2008). The requirements of managers and management are a result of the increasing size of business enterprises. As size leads to complexity, managers are needed to act as a bridge between owners and rank-and-file employees (Drucker, 2008). When ownership predefines the development direction and organizational goals, management invests their time and knowledge in executing strategies with the resources provided by ownership (Kazemian & Sanusi, 2015).

By definition, if an important role of management is to create an organizational structure that enables employees to work efficiently toward achieving organizational goals, managers are responsible for implementing and evaluating these structures through information, working with people, and taking necessary actions (Mintzberg, 2013). This is particularly evident as rank-and-file employees have transitioned from being predominantly unskilled laborers to highly educated knowledge workers (Drucker, 2008). The term "rank and file" denotes the employees in a company who are not in executive or managerial positions (Cameron & Whetten, 1983).

Additionally, Peter Drucker introduced another related concept of "knowledge worker" to refer the term of "rank and file" in his renowned publication, *The Landmarks of Tomorrow* (2023), where he characterized knowledge workers as skilled individuals who leverage theoretical and analytical knowledge obtained through formal education and training (Drucker, 2023). Knowledge workers have been steadily emerging since the 1950s, when the number of knowledge technologists in fields such as computers and manufacturing began to grow at an even faster pace (Drucker, 2008). After World War II, there was an increasing number of adults who desired to extend their learning experiences and pursue careers in the knowledge industries, and the school curriculum expanded its range of course subjects to cater these demands, including subjects such as agricultural and home economics (Tierney, 2021). Journalists serve as another prominent example of knowledge workers. The idea of improving journalism through higher education for journalists originated in the late nineteenth century in the United States (Josephi, 2019). For instance, the first journalism school in U.S. was established at the University of Missouri in 1908, offering individuals the chance to receive comprehensive education and training to acquire professional knowledge and values (The J-School/University of Missouri, n.d.). Journalism education has since expanded nationally, as evidenced by the fact that approximately 82 percent of all journalists hold a bachelor's degree ("What education do journalists have," 2023).

Management thus has become more important because knowledge is inherently specialized, and knowledge workers are characterized by their high mobility and present a greater challenge in terms of aligning them with the organization's mission (Drucker, 2008). To effectively motivate and lead knowledge workers, two-factor theory has been widely used in this approach. Two-factor theory suggests that various factors or motives can influence job satisfaction and dissatisfaction when managing knowledge workers (Herzberg, 2017). In essence, the factors that contribute to job satisfaction are different from those that contribute to job dissatisfaction. For instance, motivating factors such as achievement, recognition, and professional growth have a strong correlation with job satisfaction, while preventive factors such as salary, job security, and working conditions may impact dissatisfaction (Herzberg, 2017). A previous study examined how the two-factor theory applied in the field of the newsroom, indicating that the motivating factor of journalism professional values is a more important predictor of job satisfaction than preventative factors (Beam, 2006).

A crucial purpose for managers in motivating knowledge workers is to establish shared values that align with the objectives of the owners' missions (Drucker, 2008). The concept of shared value in the field of management was introduced by Porter and Kramer (2006). It refers to the adoption of policies and operational strategies that not only enhance a company's competitiveness but also contribute to the improvement of economic and social conditions within the communities where it operates (Porter & Kramer, 2011; Dembek et al., 2016). To achieve this purpose, managers not only need to actively lead team members to achieve organizational goals, but also to serve as facilitators, supporting team members' creative efforts (Hemlin, 2006).

Overall, conceptually, the management role can be examined in terms of three main tasks: defining the organization's specific mission, considering objectives to ensure worker productivity, and effectively managing the organization's social impacts (Drucker, 2008).

The mission of an organization goes beyond achieving business success by offering goods and services that meet consumer desires at an acceptable price point. It also involves a commitment to making a social impact or serving a purpose that extends beyond economic performance (Drucker, 2008). When setting up objectives, management objectives must closely align with the directives of the owners, necessitating constant adjustments (Chan-Olmsted, 2006; Wheelen et al., 2017). This involves activities such as "planning, organizing, integrating, measuring, and developing" (Drucker, 2008). Managers are responsible for determining goals in each objective area, building effective teams through constant communication, establishing performance targets for the organization, and playing a crucial role in the development of individuals within the organization (Drucker, 2008). Additionally, the concept of corporate social impact emphasizes the importance of organizations defining their roles in society and adhering to social and ethical standards in their business practices, which can also foster employee commitment and customer loyalty (Lindgreen & Swaen, 2010).

In sum, organizational complexity plays a key role in the importance of management (Drucker, 2008; Stacey, 1995). Knowledge workers' specialized knowledge relates to their desire for autonomy in their work. They are generally more difficult to motivate compared to manufacturing workers, and establishing shared values with owners is crucial for enhancing motivation (Dembek et al., 2016). Therefore, managers not only need to set up objectives to meet the owner's business performance mission, but also need to find common values that can be shared with knowledge workers (Drucker, 2008). Furthermore, social impact is another significant task for which managers bear responsibility. In other words, managers are accountable for maintaining high ethical standards by fostering shared values that are defined by the specialized knowledge of the industry (Lindgreen & Swaen, 2010). Thus, management needs to achieve the owners' financial goals and create an organizational culture that values the specialized knowledge, enabling the organization and its knowledge workers to fulfill their social mission.

Media Management Challenges Today

The newspaper industry is a typical case when examining the challenges of managing knowledge workers and finding a balance between offering profitable products and services while maintaining a positive social impact for the community (Picard, 2005). According to the previous scholarship in the field of newspaper journalism, the broad term of social impacts can be interpreted to mean value-based influence, such as journalism professional values and social responsibilities.

As described in Chap. 3, the norms of journalism emphasize the importance of providing a public service by delivering news that is truthful, fair, accurate, and objective (Merrill, 2012; Siebert et al., 1963). Social responsibility theory posits that a free press carries the responsibility of being accountable to society and upholding the public interest with heightened standards (Merrill, 1974; Siebert et al. 1963). Moreover, journalism serves a social function in democracy by providing information that citizens need to make informed decisions about their government and elected leaders, thereby fulfilling its social responsibilities (Kovach & Rosenstiel, 2021). These challenges have been recognized for a long time as the organizational structure of newspaper companies has become increasingly complex (Siebert et al. 1963), particularly since the 1960s when corporate newspaper ownership dominated the industry (Demers, 1996). Consequently, newspaper companies have placed greater emphasis on their economic success and, later on, the stock dividend, while paying less attention to journalism professional values, public interest, and social responsibility within a democratic society (Hollifield, 2012).

News managers are often selected from professional journalists, who are required to collaborate with other non-journalism departments, rather than being hired from management professionals (Gade, 2004).

This selection reflects the recognition of the unique nature of the newspaper industry and the value placed on journalism knowledge and professional experience (Gade, 2008). The notable point is that newspaper managers' sense of professionalism stems from journalism values.

In addition to the management challenges stemming from the unique characteristics of the industry, there are also challenges that arise from two closely related aspects of management: owners and rank-and-file employees (Drucker, 2008). These challenges include conflicts with the mission predefined by the public newspaper owner (Demers, 1996; Hollifield, 2012), as well as managing the shortage of experienced journalists to effectively achieve the organization's objectives (Reinardy, 2011, 2012; Sylvie & Gade, 2009).

News managers faced struggles related to their owners' perception of the mission, especially in the case of publicly traded newspaper ownership, when newspaper firms became accountable to the stock market. During the private ownership era, management conflicts were not apparent because private newspaper owners typically assumed the role of management due to small organizational size and simple structure (Picard & Van Weezel, 2008; Demers, 1996; Picard, 2016). However, with the advent of the public ownership era, the newspaper industry experienced rapid industry-wide expansion, with more and more newspaper companies joining the stock market in 1960s (Demers, 1996), leading to larger size and more complex structures (Hollifield, 2012). Publicly owned companies are governed by a board of directors who are not journalists, and many are not financial experts. Therefore, as long as news managers could deliver a level of profit satisfactory to the board (and maintained an attractive stock price for investors), they could prioritize their own professional (journalism) values (Galbraith, 1978; Gade, 2004). Furthermore, this rapid expansion also brought about intensified competition for the audience, or "customers," as highlighted by McManus in his book *Market-Driven Journalism* (1994). The logic of the marketplace has been embraced in many newsrooms, where a larger audience size and more entertainment-oriented content are deemed more desirable than normative journalism, which is inconsistent with the goals of public service (McManus, 1994). Meyer expressed similar concerns in his book *The Vanishing Newspaper* (2009), noting that the shifting focus from journalism quality to business performance might diminish the importance and influence of traditional newspapers in the communities they serve (Meyer, 2009). Additionally, the impacts from the capital market shifted from providing intensified financial support to imposing tremendous economic pressure, including demands for profit margins from the stock market and heavy debt burdens imposed by institutional investors (Kirchhoff, 2010). As a result of the differing preferences between profit-driven motives and a focus on journalism quality among newspaper owners and news managers, the management challenges gradually intensified (Lacy et al., 1996).

Specifically, public newspaper ownership is characterized by two distinct missions: profit-oriented and journalism-oriented (Andersson & Wiik, 2013). However, by the early twenty-first century, the digital age changed the economic dynamics of the newspaper industry, and the traditional business model broke (Picard, 2010). As a result, the adoption of an organizational strategy focused on aggressive cost control had a significant negative impact on management (Picard, 2005; Soloski, 2005). Picard (2011) observed that transitioning to a digital-only strategy could potentially reduce newspaper costs by approximately two-thirds, but this shift is not sufficient to offset the revenue loss resulting from the decline in print revenue (Picard, 2016). A study has indicated that modern audiences are generally unwilling to pay for digital content produced by traditional newsrooms (Chyi & Ng, 2020). With limited budgets and organizational resources, media management finds it challenging to maintain journalism quality (Picard, 2016). Moreover, news media managers are typically chosen from accomplished journalists who then promote and transition into managerial positions, so it is not surprising that they identify themselves as first and foremost professional journalists (Gade, 2008). As a result, another management challenge related to owners' motivation is the persistence of news managers in prioritizing journalism quality in their management approach, even when faced with demands from profit-oriented owners (Gade, 2008; Sylvie & Gade, 2009).

Additionally, newsrooms have been undergoing downsizing since the 1990s due to various factors. The primary factor is the emergence of new technologies, including initial broadcast and current internet-based media (Picard, 2011; Demers, 1996). This trend of technological development has also led to changes in audience reading behavior, with more people turning to alternative media platforms (Picard, 2011). As a result, the competitiveness of traditional newspaper circulation has diminished (Chyi & Tenenboim, 2019). Additionally, this diminished circulation has also eroded interest from the stock market (Channick, 2021; Coppins, 2021). The current reality is that the number of daily newspapers in the U.S. has experienced a significant reduction. Since 2004, the number of daily newspapers has dropped by 18 percent, from 1456 in 2004 (Gade, 2004) to 1200 in 2023, according to the most recent record (Watson, 2024).

In response to the declining number of newspapers, a significant loss has occurred in terms of experienced staff. According to the annual censuses conducted by American Society of Newspaper Editors (ASNE), there has been a drastic decline in the number of journalists working for daily newspapers in the U.S. since late 1990s when ASNE started to record the data, such as with a decrease of over 68 percent from 57,000 in 2007 to 18,020 in 2022 (ASNE, n.d.; Bureau of Labor Statistics, 2023). As a result, there has been a substantial reduction in institutional knowledge within the industry. As Drucker emphasized (2008), knowledge is a vital resource for organizations, and it is cultivated by educated and knowledgeable workers. Therefore, this decline might cause difficulties in training and guiding young journalists. For example, journalist mentoring programs have gained popularity industry-wide, especially during the first five years of a young journalist's career (Escobar, 2018). These programs provide valuable opportunities for early-career journalists to expand their professional networks and establish connections with individuals and organizations within the industry. While journalism schools often offer a range of journalism curricula and student publications for practical experience, they may not fully replicate the real-world challenges and dynamics of the industry (Blatchford, 2021). Additionally, not all young reporters attend journalism school, making the guidance and support from senior peers even more crucial in helping them navigate their careers (Escobar, 2018). However, these young professional training programs might cease to exist due to the lack of experienced journalists available as mentors.

The result of the reduced workforce is an expanded workload, particularly with the expansion of digital products (Picard, 2011). In the digital world, the publishing process is faster, and mandated no sacrifice of quality while under endless pressure to publish without any breaks (Albarran et al., 2018; Sylvie & Gade, 2009). Journalists are now required to report across multiple formats simultaneously, which has significantly increased the degree of their overwhelming workload (Lowrey & Gade, 2011). As employees adapt to new technologies, they must learn new skills and adopt new approaches to their work, resulting in an increased workload (Killebrew, 2003). Furthermore, studies conducted by Reinardy (2011, 2012) on burnout in journalism have revealed that editors and journalists frequently face negative working attitudes attributed to extrinsic factors such as excessive workload and uncertain job security. In other words, these types of preventative factors have gained increasing influence in the current uncertain working environment, particularly in relation to their impact on journalism job satisfaction.

In order to address these challenges, news managers must implement various management strategies (Sylvie & Gade, 2009). For example, when it comes to producing different media products (print and digital) within a single newsroom, news managers need to effectively assign relevance and timelines based on various situational contexts, which includes considerations such as information format, system proximity, and other factors (Adam et al., 2002). Moreover, encouraging creative ideas and fostering innovation is crucial for the survival of an organization. As emphasized by Schumpeter, the capacity to adjust and thrive in a dynamic environment is crucial for the success of organizations (1965). Innovation functions as a catalyst for both growth and renewal, increasing the adaptive capabilities of the firm (Uhl-Bien & Arena, 2018). Journalism, due to its reliance on storytelling, writing, and visual communication, is inherently a creative profession. However, when staff are stretched thin and under-resourced, and employees experience anxiety over job security and burnout, it becomes much more difficult to encourage and manage employee creativity (Besemer & O'Quin, 1999; also see Sylvie & Gade, 2009).

In summary, the dual mission of public newspaper ownership, encompassing both journalism-oriented and profit-oriented goals, has given rise to various management challenges (Andersson & Wiik, 2013; Demers, 1996). News managers face the task of effectively allocating limited organizational resources to balance these different missions, while also navigating the rapid pace of digital transformation (Picard, 2011, 2016). These challenges make it difficult for managers to establish clear objectives and effectively manage their rank-and-file employees. Additionally, the acquisition of newspapers by hedge funds further exacerbates these challenges because hedge fund ownership primarily focuses on immediate financial returns, rather than long-term development and value creation (Morgenson & Rosner, 2023).

Media Management Challenges: Future with Hedge Fund Ownership

As explored in the previous chapter, hedge fund ownership presents significant threats due to its aggressive harvesting actions, with hedge funds often referred to as "money-spinning machines" or "plunderers" (Morgenson & Rosner, 2023, p. 3). Unlike traditional investors who aim for the long-term health and profitability of companies, hedge funds adopt a short-term profit return strategy and often take full control of the companies they acquire with the intention of maximizing profit quickly (Andrew & Ayako, 2010; Morgenson & Rosner, 2023).

In fact, the hedge fund industry is the fastest growing sector in the U.S., outpacing the economic growth of all other sectors, according to a recent report that was made by IBISWorld ("Hedge Funds in the US," 2023). The market size of the hedge funds industry in the U.S. has grown at an average rate of 6.4 percent per year between 2017 and 2022, and it was expected to grow by 3.5 percent in 2023, with a projected profit margin of 40 percent (Yahoo Finance, 2023). While the impact of hedge fund ownership on management is a relatively new research area in the newspaper industry, many studies have been conducted in other industries.

Broadly speaking, hedge funds target undervalued public companies that are vulnerable in the stock market (Andrew & Ayako, 2010; Stulz,

2007). An undervalued stock refers to a situation where its market price is considerably lower than its perceived intrinsic value, which is often derived from the company's tangible assets (Khartit, 2020). However, it is important to note that the purpose of such acquisitions is not to rescue the acquired companies; instead, these acquisitions often create additional challenges for the acquired companies, making it more difficult for them to thrive (Morgenson & Rosner, 2023). As typical financial institutions, hedge funds often borrow money at short-term, high interest rates from partners or clients and target undervalued public companies in the stock market (Stulz, 2007). In order to meet the interest payments on the debt and recoup the acquisition costs, hedge funds typically employ strategies that involve quickly gutting the acquired company (Coppins, 2021). This may include selling off assets or business divisions and implementing cost-cutting measures such as employee layoffs and reductions in healthcare and retirement benefits (Morgenson & Rosner, 2023). According to a study by Ayash and Rastad (2021), 20 percent of companies taken over by these firms ended up filing for bankruptcy, which is ten times higher than the failure rates observed in other types of acquisitions. However, the failures do not always harm the acquirers, as they often legally insulate themselves from the financial consequences faced by the companies that fall into bankruptcy (Morgenson & Rosner, 2023).

In addition, hedge funds are motivated to minimize risks and maximize profits, functioning as profit-generating engines within the companies they acquire (Morgenson & Rosner, 2023). For instance, hedge funds often target undervalued public companies in well-developed industries that have undergone significant organizational change, such as those on the brink of bankruptcy (Andrew & Ayako, 2010; Stulz, 2007). Hedge funds typically employ two strategies for risk management: fully controlling the business they acquired and eliminating any self-interest of management, or quickly selling off tangible resources for monetary gain (Stulz, 2007). Moreover, it is important to consider that news managers as professional journalists are primarily guided by their professional values and sense of journalism professionalism (Gade, 2008). In short, the management implications can be examined through the lens of value-based influence or so-called social impacts and organizational resource support.

Value-based influences on news media management include journalism professional values, public interest that serves a democratic function, and social responsibility (Siebert et al. 1963). Specifically, journalism professional values have long been regarded as foundational principles that should take precedence over economic gain in the field of journalism (Weaver et al., 2009). The primary function of a newspaper is to serve the public interest by ensuring that citizens are well-informed, which in turn benefits democracy, as it enables citizens to actively participate in guiding the governance of their country (Kovach & Rosenstiel, 2021). Proponents of social responsibility theory argue that media should prioritize promoting the public interest over their own economic considerations (Siebert et al. 1963). These values are often considered difficult to measure in monetary terms (Benson et al., 2018; Lacy & Rosenstiel, 2015). However, in the context of hedge fund ownership, any actions that deviate from the predetermined organizational goals are often viewed as self-interest and are required to be minimized (Bansal, 2013; Bratton, 2008). This ultimately poses a threat to the newspaper's ability to fulfill its democratic mission of serving the public.

Another potential management challenge arises in the aspect of organizational resource support. Hedge funds target undervalued public companies with the belief that the economic value of their tangible resources exceeds their market value, presenting an opportunity for profitable asset sales (Andrew & Ayako, 2010; Stulz, 2007). Tangible resources in the newspaper industry typically include physical workplaces and human resources (Chan-Olmsted, 2006; Massey, 2016). However, hedge funds often sell tangible assets, such as newspaper properties, buildings, publishing and distributing equipment, and reduce intangible assets, including work forces, high-salaried employees, and institutional knowledge, etc. These challenges include widespread layoffs, which have led to overwhelming workloads for journalists and contributed to a high incidence of stress. Additionally, the relocation of news organizations from expensive downtown areas to cheap suburban locations has resulted in reduced proximity to key news sources, further exacerbating the difficulties faced by journalists in their work (Usher, 2015). Therefore, the aggressive harvesting actions of hedge funds in the sale of tangible resources could pose an even greater threat. For instance, similar cases have arisen in the healthcare industry. When private equity firms acquired hospitals and nursing homes, they promptly reduced staffing levels by replacing qualified and experienced professionals with less trained and cheaper alternatives (Bos & Harrington, 2017; Morgenson & Rosner, 2023). Studies have shown that nursing homes owned by private equity firms experienced a 10 percent higher rate of resident deaths compared to facilities not owned by private equity from 2005 to 2017 (Scott, 2021). The proportion of nursing homes owned by private equity has increased significantly, reaching around 11 percent by 2021 (Knight, 2022).

Furthermore, as financial equities, hedge funds exert full control over the public companies they acquire, resulting in a shift from public to private status (Stulz, 2007). Converting the acquired public company into a private entity provides the new owners with increased control over the company's operations and enables them to bypass various regulatory obligations, including those related to public awareness of their profits, financial condition, as well as their motives and goals (Balasubramanian & James, 2022). Without the scrutiny associated with public ownership, media management challenges may intensify and become harder to address.

In sum, under hedge fund ownership, two primary approaches can guide the consideration of media management challenges in the future: value-based issues and resource support (Andrew & Ayako, 2010; Morgenson & Rosner, 2023; Stulz, 2007). Specifically, hedge funds, functioning as "money-spinning machines," exercise full control over the governance of the companies they acquire, which often leads to swift disposal of physical assets and extensive layoffs (Morgenson & Rosner, 2023). Consequently, newspapers are perceived as no different from other public businesses, resulting in the devaluation of intangible resources such as professional values, public interest, and social responsibilities, as these are considered to have no immediate contribution to profit returns according to hedge funds (Andrew & Ayako, 2010). Ultimately, hedge fund ownership exacerbates existing media management challenges within the newspaper industry and poses a significant threat to the journalism norms rooted in democracy, which aims to provide citizens with necessary information (Benson et al., 2018; Coppins, 2021).

Summary

This chapter reviews the roles of management in the newspaper industry and its relationship with ownership. It specifically explores the historic friction between management having to balance financial goals of owners and public service rooted in journalism' sense of professionalism, and how this friction emerged during public ownership era and has become more acute under hedge fund ownership. Additionally, it highlights the conflict that arises between newspaper hedge fund owners and professional managers who primarily identify themselves as journalists. In essence, the newspaper ownership change to hedge funds further exacerbates this news management conflict.

Organizational structural complexity plays a significant role in creating management challenges, particularly in positions that involve managing knowledge workers with specialized expertise and an expanded ownership mission in business performance (Drucker, 2008). In the context of the newspaper industry, news media managers face unique challenges in addition to the common management issues. These challenges arise from the function of journalism norms, which involves providing information and public service to the communities they serve (Merrill, 2012; Siebert et al., 1963). Unlike managers in other industries, news media managers often have a professional journalism identity that aligns them more closely with the value-based side of their work (Gade, 2008). They prioritize the principles of journalism over solely focusing on business performance (Sylvie & Gade, 2009). This can create tension between the journalistic mission and the financial objectives of the organization.

The assumption was that during the early stage of the public ownership period, before the emergence of digital media as competitors, high-quality journalism products from newspapers generated higher profits that satisfied both the stock market and public owners (Demers, 1996). However, with the rapid development and influence of digital media, this assumption no longer holds true (Picard, 2010). Digital media have captured the interests of the audience, advertisers, and the stock market, leading to conflicts in management within the newspaper industry. Moreover, when examining the change in owners' motivations, management conflicts can be complex. When ownership and news media management both value journalism quality, the management issues often revolve around sustainability and other long-term developments, such as restructuring the newsroom to increase the efficient production procedures (Gade, 2008) or diversifying media product portfolios (Picard, 2005); in contrast, when owners excessively focus on profit-driven objectives, short-term management decisions are more likely to be made, such as cost control measures and limited resources support (Lacy et al., 1996). These decisions can have a negative impact on news media management, leading to issues like burnout among managers (Reinardy, 2011, 2012).

Hedge fund ownership will extend existing challenges and likely create greater conflict between news managers and their owners. Hedge funds typically prioritize immediate profit return strategies and are less concerned about long-term development or sustainability (Stulz, 2007). Their focus is primarily on achieving quick money back through the sale of tangible resources (Morgenson & Rosner, 2023). As a result, there is a high probability that hedge fund ownership may undermine journalism's professional values and social responsibility as crucial elements of journalism norms in a democratic system.

In short, with the ongoing shift in newspaper ownership from public to hedge fund, the implications for news management are predominantly centered around the organizational level. As Drucker (2008) claimed, the major tasks of management in a knowledge industry involve aligning with the owners' mission, setting operational objectives with rank-and-file employees, and maintaining social impacts.

Research Questions

Study One

RQ1: What are the long-term performances of the P/E ratio of the four public U.S. newspaper companies from 2007 to 2022?

RQ2: What are the long-term performances of the free cash flow of the four public U.S. newspaper companies from 2007 to 2022?

RQ3: What are the long-term performances of the tangible resources of the four public U.S. newspaper companies from 2007 to 2022?

A: What are the long-term performances of the employee-related tangible resources of the four public U.S. newspaper companies from 2007 to 2022?

    A-1: What has been the change of the total number of employees of the four public U.S. newspaper companies from 2007 to 2022?
    A-2: What has been the change of the expenses for employee wages and benefits of the four public U.S. newspaper companies from 2007 to 2022?
    A-3: What has been the percentage change of the employee-related expenses out of the total operational expenses of the four public U.S. newspaper companies from 2007 to 2022?

B: What are the long-term performances of the property-related tangible resources of the four public U.S. newspaper companies from 2007 to 2022?

    B-1: What has been the change in the value at cost of property-related assets of the four public U.S. newspaper companies from 2007 to 2022?
    B-2: What has been the percentage change in the value at cost of property-related assets out of the total assets of the four public U.S. newspaper companies from 2007 to 2022?
    B-3: What has been the change in the value at cost of land and buildings specifically of the four public U.S. newspaper companies from 2007 to 2022?

RQ4: When and what specific types of corporate transactions occurred in the four public U.S. newspaper companies from 2007 to 2022?

A: When did specific corporate spin-off transaction strategies occur in the four public U.S. newspaper companies from 2007 to 2022?

B: When did specific corporate merge transaction strategies occur in the four public U.S. newspaper companies from 2007 to 2022?

C: When did specific corporate bankruptcy transaction strategies occur in the four public U.S. newspaper companies from 2007 to 2022?

Study Two

RQ5: What perceptions do news managers of hedge fund-owned newspapers have regarding newspaper missions under hedge fund ownership?

  A: What perceptions do news managers of hedge fund-owned newspapers have regarding the mission of journalism quality under hedge fund ownership?
  B: What perceptions do news managers of hedge fund-owned newspapers have regarding the mission of profit-driven motivation under hedge fund ownership?

RQ6: What perceptions do news managers of hedge fund-owned newspapers have regarding operational objectives under hedge fund ownership?

  A: What perceptions do news managers of hedge fund-owned newspapers have regarding the objective of young journalists training under hedge fund ownership?
  B: What perceptions do news managers of hedge fund-owned newspapers have regarding the objective of allocating overwhelming workload under hedge fund ownership?

RQ7: What perceptions do news managers of hedge fund-owned newspapers have regarding maintaining social impacts under hedge fund ownership?

  A: What perceptions do news managers of hedge fund-owned newspapers have regarding the social impact of journalism professional values under hedge fund ownership?

B: What perceptions do news managers of hedge fund-owned newspapers have regarding the social impact of public interest under hedge fund ownership?

C: What perceptions do news managers of hedge fund-owned newspapers have regarding the social impact of social responsibilities under hedge fund ownership?

References

Adam, B., Whipp, R., & Sabelis, I. (2002). Choreographing time and management: Traditions. In *Making time: Time and management in modern organizations* (pp. 1–28). Oxford University Press.

Albarran, A. B., Mierzejewska, B., & Jung, J. (Eds.). (2018). *Handbook of media management and economics*. Routledge.

Andersson, U., & Wiik, J. (2013). Journalism meets management: Changing leadership in Swedish news organizations. *Journalism Practice, 7*(6), 705–719.

Andrew, M., & Ayako, Y. (2010). The economics of private equity funds. *The Review of Financial Studies, 3*, 26.

ASNE (n.d.). *The American Society of News Editors*. News Leaders Association. Retrieved from: https://members.newsleaders.org/about-us

Ayash, B., & Rastad, M. (2021). Leveraged buyouts and financial distress. *Finance Research Letters, 38*, 101452.

Balasubramanian, K., & James, M. (2022, November). What are the advantages and disadvantages of a company going public? *Investopedia.* https://www.investopedia.com/ask/answers/advantages-disadvantages-company-going-public/

Bansal, P. (2013). Inducing frame-breaking insights through qualitative research. *Corporate Governance: An International Review, 21*(2), 127–130.

Beam, R. A. (2006). Organizational goals and priorities and the job satisfaction of US. Journalists. *Journalism & Mass Communication Quarterly, 83*(1), 169–185.

Benson, R., Neff, T., & Hessérus, M. (2018). Media ownership and public service news: How strong are institutional logics? *The International Journal of Press/Politics, 23*(3), 275–298.

Besemer, S. P., & O'Quin, K. (1999). Confirming the three-factor creative product analysis matrix model in an American sample. *Creativity Research Journal, 12*(4), 287–296.

Blatchford, T. (2021, August). How students and early career journalists can approach potential mentors with intention and respect. *Poynter.* https://www.poynter.org/educators-students/2021/how-students-and-early-career-journalists-can-approach-potential-mentors-with-intention-and-respect/

Bos, A., & Harrington, C. (2017). What happens to a nursing home chain when private equity takes over? A longitudinal case study. *INQUIRY: The Journal of Health Care Organization, Provision, and Financing, 54*, 0046958017742761.

Bratton, W. W. (2008). Private equity's three lessons for agency theory. *European Business Organization Law Review (EBOR), 9*(4), 509–533.

Bureau of Labor Statistics. (2023). 27-3023 news analysts, reporters, and journalists. https://www.bls.gov/oes/current/oes273023.htm

Cameron, K. S., & Whetten, D. A. (1983). Models of the organizational life cycle: Applications to higher education. *The Review of Higher Education, 6*(4), 269–299.

Channick, R. (2021, May). Tribune Publishing offering buyouts to newsroom employees, two days after purchase by hedge fund Alden. *Chicago Tribune.* https://www.chicagotribune.com/business/ct-biz-tribune-publishing-newsroom-buyouts-alden-20210526-ihthwykitjfmrpnj63whhlqw5i-story.html

Chan-Olmsted, S. M. (2006). *Competitive strategy for media firms: Strategic and brand management in changing media markets.* Routledge.

Chyi, H. I., & Ng, Y. M. M. (2020). Still unwilling to pay: An empirical analysis of 50 US newspapers' digital subscription results. *Digital Journalism, 8*(4), 526–547.

Chyi, H. I., & Tenenboim, O. (2019). Charging more and wondering why readership declined? A longitudinal study of US newspapers' price hikes, 2008–2016. *Journalism Studies, 20*(14), 2113–2129.

Coppins, M. (2021, October). A secretive hedge fund is gutting newsrooms. *The Atlantic.* https://www.theatlantic.com/magazine/archive/2021/11/alden-global-capital-killing-americas-newspapers/620171/

Dembek, K., Singh, P., & Bhakoo, V. (2016). Literature review of shared value: A theoretical concept or a management buzzword? *Journal of Business Ethics, 137*, 231–267.

Demers, D. (1996). Corporate newspaper structure, editorial page vigor, and social change. *Journalism & Mass Communication Quarterly, 73*(4), 857–877.

Drucker, P. (2008). Introduction: Management and managers defined; management as a social function and liberal art; knowledge is all. *Management,* 1–25.

Drucker, P. (2023). *Landmarks of Tomorrow: A report on the new post modern world*. Routledge.

Escobar, N. (2018, February). How do young journalists get their training? *ProPublica*. https://www.propublica.org/article/ask-ppil-how-do-young-journalists-get-their-training

Gade, P. J. (2004). Newspapers and organizational development: Management and journalist perceptions of newsroom cultural change. *Journalism & Communication Monographs, 6*(1), 3–55.

Gade, P. J. (2008). Journalism guardians in a time of great change: Newspaper editors' perceived influence in integrated news organizations. *Journalism & Mass Communication Quarterly, 85*(2), 371–392.

Galbraith, J. K. (1978). On post Keynesian economics. *Journal of Post Keynesian Economics, 1*(1), 8–11.

Gedajlovic, E. R., & Shapiro, D. M. (1998). Management and ownership effects: Evidence from five countries. *Strategic Management Journal, 19*(6), 533–553.

Hedge Funds in the US-Market Size 2004–2029. (2023, April). *IBISWorld*. https://www.ibisworld.com/industry-statistics/market-size/hedge-funds-united-states/

Hemlin, S. (2006). Creative knowledge environments for research groups in biotechnology. The influence of leadership and organizational support in universities and business companies. *Scientometrics, 67*(1), 121–142.

Herzberg, F. (2017). *Motivation to work*. Routledge.

Hollifield, A. (2012). Changing perceptions of organizations. *Changing the news: The forces shaping journalism in uncertain times*, pp. 193–212.

Josephi, B. (2019). Journalism education. In *The Handbook of Journalism Studies* (pp. 55–69). Routledge.

The J-School/University of Missouri. (n.d.). *Mission and Strategic Plan*. University of Missouri. Retrieved from: https://journalism.missouri.edu/

Kazemian, S., & Sanusi, Z. M. (2015). Earnings management and ownership structure. *Procedia Economics and Finance, 31*, 618–624.

Khartit, K. (2020, December). Undervalued. *Investopedia*. https://www.investopedia.com/terms/u/undervalued.asp

Killebrew, K. C. (2003). Culture, creativity and convergence: Managing journalists in a changing information workplace. *International Journal on Media Management, 5*(1), 39–46.

Kirchhoff, S. M. (2010). *US newspaper industry in transition* (Vol. 40700). Congressional Research Service.

Knight, V. (2022, April). Private equity ownership of nursing homes triggers capitol hill questions – And a GAO probe. *KFF Health News*. https://kffhealthnews.org/news/article/private-equity-ownership-of-nursing-homes-triggers-federal-probe/

Kovach, B., & Rosenstiel, T. (2021). *The elements of journalism, revised and updated 4th edition: What newspeople should know and the public should expect*. Crown Publishing Group.

Lacy, S., & Rosenstiel, T. (2015). *Defining and measuring quality journalism*. Rutgers School of Communication and Information.

Lacy, S., Shaver, M. A., & Cyr, C. S. (1996). The effects of public ownership and newspaper competition on the financial performance of newspaper corporations: A replication and extension. *Journalism & Mass Communication Quarterly*, *73*(2), 332–341.

Lindgreen, A., & Swaen, V. (2010). Corporate social responsibility. *International Journal of Management Reviews*, *12*(1), 1–7.

Lowrey, W., & Gade, P. J. (2011). *Changing the news*. Routledge.

Massey, B. L. (2016). Resource-based analysis of the survival of independent web-native news ventures. *Journalism & Mass Communication Quarterly*, *93*(4), 770–788.

McManus, J. H. (1994). *Market-driven journalism: Let the citizen beware?* Sage Publications.

Merrill, J. C. (1974). *The imperative of freedom: A philosophy of journalistic autonomy*.

Merrill, J. (2012). Journalism and democracy. *Changing the news: The forces shaping journalism in uncertain times*, pp. 45–62.

Meyer, P. (2009). *The vanishing newspaper: Saving journalism in the information age*. University of Missouri Press.

Mintzberg, H. (2013). *Simply managing: What managers do – And can do better*. Berrett-Koehler Publishers.

Morgenson, G., & Rosner, J. (2023). *These are the plunderers: How private equity runs – And Wrecks – America*. Simon and Schuster.

Picard, R. G. (Ed.). (2005). *Corporate governance of media companies*. Jönköping Internat. Business School.

Picard, R. G. (2010). The future of the news industry. *Media and society*, *5*, 365–379.

Picard, R. G. (2011). *The economics and financing of media companies*. Fordham University Press.

Picard, R. G. (2016). Isolated and particularised: The state of contemporary media and communications policy research. *Javnost-The Public, 23*(2), 135–152.

Picard, R. G., & Van Weezel, A. (2008). Capital and control: Consequences of different forms of newspaper ownership. *The International Journal on Media Management, 10*(1), 22–31.

Porter, M. E., & Kramer, M. R. (2006). The link Between Competitive advantage and corporate social responsibility. *Harvard Business Review, 84*(12), 78–92.

Porter, M. E., & Kramer, M. R. (2011). How to reinvent capitalism—and unleash a wave of innovation and growth. *Manag Sustain Bus*, 323.

Reinardy, S. (2011). Newspaper journalism in crisis: Burnout on the rise, eroding young journalists' career commitment. *Journalism, 12*(1), 33–50.

Reinardy, S. (2012). Job security, satisfaction influence work commitment. *Newspaper Research Journal, 33*(1), 54–70.

Scott, G. (2021, October). Delisting. *Investopedia*. https://www.investopedia.com/terms/d/delisting.asp

Siebert, F., Peterson, T., & Schramm, W. (1963). *Four theories of the press: The authoritarian, libertarian, social responsibility, and Soviet communist concepts of what the press should be and do*. University of Illinois press.

Soloski, J. (2005). Taking stock redux: Corporate ownership and journalism of publicly traded newspaper companies. In *Corporate governance of media companies* (pp. 59–76). Jönköping International Business School.

Stacey, R. D. (1995). The science of complexity: An alternative perspective for strategic change processes. *Strategic Management Journal, 16*(6), 477–495.

Stulz, R. M. (2007). Hedge funds: Past, present, and future. *Journal of Economic Perspectives, 21*(2), 175–194.

Sylvie, G., & Gade, P. (2009). Changes in news work: Implications for newsroom managers. *Journal of Media Business Studies, 6*(1), 113–148.

Tierney, W. (2021, April). What should higher Ed learn from World War II? *Inside Higher ED*. https://www.insidehighered.com/views/2021/04/05/higher-ed-should-learn-lessons-world-war-ii-about-serving-public-good-opinion#:~:text=After%20World%20War%20II%2C%20American,financially%20hammered%20by%20the%20war.

Uhl-Bien, M., & Arena, M. (2018). Leadership for organizational adaptability: A theoretical synthesis and integrative framework. *The Leadership Quarterly, 29*(1), 89–104.

Usher, N. (2015). Newsroom moves and the newspaper crisis evaluated: Space, place, and cultural meaning. *Media, Culture & Society, 37*(7), 1005–1021.

Watson, A. (2024, December). Number of local daily and non-daily newspapers in publication in the United States from 2004 to 2023. *Statista*. https://www.statista.com/statistics/944134/number-closed-merged-newspapers/

Weaver, D. H., Beam, R. A., Brownlee, B. J., Voakes, P. S., & Wilhoit, G. C. (2009). *The American journalist in the 21st century: US news people at the dawn of a new millennium*. Routledge.

What Education Do Journalists Have? (2023). *CareerExplorer*. https://www.careerexplorer.com/careers/journalist/education/

Wheelen, T. L., Hunger, J. D., Hoffman, A. N., & Bamford, C. E. (2017). Strategic management and business policy (p. 55).

Whitney, J., McMahon, A., & Richard, J. (2021, November). Local news deserts are expanding: Here's what we'll lose. *Washington Post*. https://www.washingtonpost.com/magazine/interactive/2021/local-news-deserts-expanding/

Yahoo Finance. (2023). https://finance.yahoo.com/quote/GCI/

5

Methods

Abstract Two sequential studies were conducted. In brief, a longitudinal content analysis of corporate annual reports assessed the vulnerability of the daily newspaper industry to attacks from hedge funds, leading to in-depth interviews of news managers on impact of hedge fund ownership on daily newspaper organizations.

Keywords In-depth interview • Annual reports • Snowball sampling • Daily newspaper organizations • News managers

Specifically, Study One involved a content analysis to examine the vulnerability of publicly traded newspaper companies, and the factors that influence hedge funds to take acquisition actions. Actually, the entire daily newspaper industry is vulnerable due to increasing competition from digital media and the uncertain economic environment since the twenty-first century (Picard, 2011), and hedge funds often target the industry level to concentrate their expertise and reduce risks (Brav et al., 2015; Morgenson & Rosner, 2023). Thus, all public newspaper companies or firms could potentially be targets for hedge funds.

Three main factors or variable categories are usually explored by hedge funds, as well as in this study, which are P/E ratio, free cash flow, tangible resources (Stulz, 2007). The primary related data sources that are utilized by hedge funds are companies' annual reports (Stulz, 2007), which Study One focused on. An annual report is a legal corporate document that disseminates the public organization's corporate business information to its shareholders in the U.S. (Hayes, 2023). These reports are required to be filed for all publicly traded companies by the U.S. Securities and Exchange Commission (SEC) (SEC.gov, n.d.).

Hedge funds have recently launched fierce attacks on some public newspaper companies. The study population includes two existing organizations that have been attacked by hedge funds multiple times—Gannett and Lee Enterprises—and two companies that have been purchased through leveraged buyouts by hedge funds—Tribune Publishing and McClatchy. In short, the analysis included newspaper companies that have experience with hedge funds.

In Study Two, by examining the impacts of hedge fund ownership on the value and importance of news management, this study explored the conflict created between hedge fund directives driven by purely short-term profit motives, journalism values rooted in public service, and a democratic mission. Building upon the results from Study One, news management efficiency should be challenged by the increasing financial pressure and the competitive digital environment (Picard, 2011). According to Drucker's perspective on managing knowledge workers (2008), the main management routine tasks include clarifying the owners' mission, establishing objectives for rank-and-file employees, and evaluating social impacts.

Study Two utilized an in-depth interview approach with news managers from newspaper companies currently owned by hedge funds, including Tribune Publishing, which was acquired in 2021 (Coppins, 2021), and McClatchy, which was acquired in 2019 (Hall, 2020). The in-depth interview allows participants to articulate and elaborate on their comprehensive perspectives (Denzin & Lincoln, 2008). Even though more public newspaper companies have been threatened by hedge funds' aggressive attacks, the ownership impacts have stayed at the organizational level and haven't reached the management operational level. For example, Gannett survived a hostile hedge fund takeover attempt in 2019 from the stock market and kept their more than two hundred daily newspapers still under its public ownership (Lee, 2019).

In short, for the research population, Study One, consisting of content analysis on annual reports, covered the public companies that have recently been targeted by hedge funds: Gannett, Lee Enterprises, Tribune Publishing, and McClatchy. Study Two, involving in-depth interviews, focused on the news managers with direct experience and perspectives of hedge fund ownership from Tribune Publishing and McClatchy. The following section will introduce the total four newspaper companies in detail.

Four U.S. Corporate Newspaper Companies

All of these newspaper companies are well-established with a long history of development and have been recognized for maintaining high journalistic standards, as well as undergoing various economic uncertainties and challenges. In recent years, four out of seven public daily newspaper companies have become targets of hedge funds. The remaining publicly traded newspaper companies that haven't been attacked by hedge funds are New York Times, News Corp, and DallasNews Corporation.

Gannett Company was formed in 1923 by Frank Gannett. In 2019, New Media Investment Group (Legacy New Media) completed its acquisition of Gannett Co., Inc, and merged its GateHouse media into it, making Gannett the largest newspaper publisher in the U.S. Its current media portfolio includes 217 daily newspapers across 45 states in the U.S., comprising their flagship national newspaper *USA TODAY* (VA), as well as various local media organizations such as *Detroit Free Press* (MI), *The Arizona Republic* (AZ), and *The Oklahoman* (OK). Gannett newsrooms have been awarded a total of 96 Pulitzer Prizes, including the most recent one—the 2020 Pulitzer Prize for breaking news reporting (Gannett Annual Report, 2022).

USA TODAY was launched in 1982 and now also serves as the cornerstone of the Gannett newsroom network, known as the USA TODAY

NETWORK. This network enables content sharing capabilities across both local and national markets (Gannett Annual Report, 2015).

In 2019, Gannett successfully withstood an aggressive attack from Alden hedge fund through its wholly-owned subsidiary, MNG Enterprises (Lee, 2019).

Lee Enterprises is a local news provider that was founded in 1890 and incorporated in 1950. Currently, Lee is operates in 47 mid-sized markets in the U.S., such as *St. Louis Post-Dispatch* (MO), *Omaha World Herald* (NE), and *Buffalo News* (NY) (Lee Enterprises Annual Report, 2022).

In 2011, Lee filed for bankruptcy (Reuters, 2011). However, in 2012, Warren Buffett paid off Lee's debt and supported the company's return to the capital market through his own media group, Berkshire Hathaway Inc. (BH) (Snider, 2020). After eight years of Buffett's involvement and support, Lee acquired BH media group in 2020 with Warren Buffett's agreement, using cash (Snider, 2020).

In the capital market, Lee resisted an attack from hedge fund Alden Global Capital in 2022 (Mansouri, 2022). Alden attempted to acquire Lee through the common stock market, and in response, Lee's board of directors implemented a shareholder rights plan, commonly known as a "poison pill," to defend against this attack (Mullin, 2021).

Tribune Publishing was spun off as an independent company on August 4, 2014, from Tribune Media Company (Tribune Publishing Annual Report, 2020).

Chicago Tribune Media Group serves as the flagship business segment within Tribune Publishing and acts as the primary source for content creation and distribution for Tribune's other local media groups, such as California News Group and the Sun Sentinel Media Group (Tribune Publishing Annual Report, 2020). Overall, Tribune Publishing has earned a combined total of 65 Pulitzer Prizes, including awards in 2020.

Regarding Tribune Publishing's business structure, it underwent a reorganization and began managing operations through two distinct segments, labeled as M and X, from 2016 until 2021 before the acquisition. Particularly, segment M's product mix consists of three types of publications: daily/weekly newspapers such as *Chicago Tribune* (IL), weekly newspapers such as *Hoy San Diego* (CA), and niche publications and direct mail; Segment X focuses on the company's digital productions such as www.tronc.com and www.sun-sentinel.com, which encompass digital revenues and related expenses across Tribune's diverse portfolio (Tribune Publishing Annual Report, 2021).

Hedge fund Alden Global Capital successfully acquired Tribune Publishing for a total of $635 million, and this acquisition received final approval on May 21, 2021, and was officially completed on May 25, 2021 (Coppins, 2021). Because this company has been delisted, annual reports were no longer published starting from 2021.

McClatchy Company was formed in Sacramento, California in 1857, and the McClatchy family took full ownership since 1883 (McClatchy Company Records, n.d.). It is dedicated to being a provider of local news. The McClatchy Company offers local journalism to 30 communities across with 14 states (McClatchy Annual Report, 2019), including prominent newspapers such as the *Miami Herald* (FL) and *The Kansas City Star* (MO).

McClatchy took the voluntary step of filing petitions for reorganization under Chapter 11 of the U.S. Bankruptcy Code on February 13, 2020. Subsequently, hedge fund Chatham Asset Management acquired McClatchy for $312 million in cash in 2020 (Hall, 2020). Since this public company was acquired by a private firm (hedge fund) in 2020, the financial report has not been required by the SEC to be published (SEC.gov, n.d.).

Study One Measures—Longitudinal Content Analysis

Most publicly traded newspaper companies in the U.S. have undergone a hundred years of development, and the manifestation of their success and failure also requires a considerable amount of time. Therefore, a long-term observation is necessary to understand why and how they became vulnerable to the market. A longitudinal study as this research technique involves studying the same group over time (Caruana et al., 2015). The quantitative content analysis method effectively reveals patterns in extensive datasets with reliability and validity (Riffe, et al., 2019).

Publicly traded newspaper companies' annual reports served as the primary dataset for this study because they provide comprehensive information about the companies' financial statements and corporate strategies (Kenton, 2020; Martin, 1998).

For the observation period, the 2008 recession was a significant turning point in U.S. economic history that prompted various industries, including the newspaper industry, to undergo substantial or complete business landscape changes (Chyi & Tenenboim, 2019). Beyond the recession, the evolving digital environment has further challenged the newspaper industry's opportunities for rebound. The rise of social media and the preponderance of new digital media outlets have led to increased competition and a greater number of advertising platforms within the media ecosystem (Picard, 2011). This shift has disrupted the industry's longstanding reliance on print advertising—the traditional business model (Picard, 2011). Consequently, the years following 2008 have become progressively more challenging. Therefore, this study examined annual reports starting from 2007—the year before 2008 up to the most recent year with available published annual reports, which is 2022.

In summary, this longitudinal content analysis study spanned a period of 16 years, from 2007 to 2022, and covered four newspaper companies' annual reports. While the existing publicly traded newspaper companies have generated their annual reports on time, two former companies did not do so. Tribune Publishing became an individual publicly traded newspaper company only in 2013 and ceased to be publicly traded in 2021. Similarly, McClatchy ended its activities in the stock market since 2020 due to its ownership changing from publicly traded to privately owned by hedge funds (Hall, 2020). This change indicates that annual reports are no longer needed to be generated as a private firm. As a result, the total number of available annual reports for Study One was 55, including 16 from Gannett, 16 from Lee, 9 from Tribune Publishing, and 14 from McClatchy.

Annual Report Variables

Regarding the variables to be collected from newspaper companies' annual reports, the content analysis encompassed two types of data. First, numerical data involved number-based variables, including P/E ratio, free cash flow, tangible resources (employee wages & physical property at cost). In the evaluation of hedge funds, undervalued companies should be the ones with low P/E ratios, low or unstable free cash flow performance, and a high portion of tangible resources. Second, a thematic analysis focused on the variables of corporate transaction strategies, including spin-offs, mergers, and bankruptcies (Stulz, 2007). These strategies hold strong reference value for being signals for hedge funds, as companies are likely to have the least resistance to outside attacks during such moments (Stulz, 2007).

P/E Ratio

The P/E ratio is obtained by "dividing the market value price per share by the company's earnings per share" (Murphy, 2023). P/E ratio is a crucial indicator that determines whether a company's stock is either overvalued or undervalued (Murphy, 2023). As the formula for the P/E ratio shows: P/E=stock price/earnings per share, an elevated P/E ratio could suggest that the stock's price is comparatively high in relation to its earnings per share, potentially signifying overvaluation; conversely, a low P/E ratio may imply that the current stock price is relatively low compared to its earnings per share (Murphy, 2023). Moreover, stockholders and investors usually consider additional external indicators to support their predictions for the company's future development, such as the financial performance of other public companies in the same industry or the S&P 500 index in general.

Therefore, although the price per share (P) and earnings per share (E) are listed in the company's annual reports, no company posts the specific P/E ratio in their annual reports. Instead, many professional financial institutions provide the P/E ratio for public companies, with the most authoritative source being Yahoo Finance (Zucchi, 2022). While there are several financial analysis platforms accessible to the general public, Yahoo Finance is renowned for providing more accurate real-time stock market data and more comprehensive expert analysis (Zucchi, 2022).

Free Cash Flow

The free cash flow indicates the amount of cash remaining after operating and investing expenses have been paid (Wagner, 2022). The annual reports break down operating expenses and investing expenses as different categories listed in the financial statement of Free Cash Flow. Operating expenses include the expenses for production, human resources, administration, and acquisition activities; while investing expenses include the expenses for financing, debt, and stock activities (Wagner, 2022). The ability to keep some cash on hand can determine the company's economic health, but it doesn't necessarily reflect the income they earn—profit (Fernando, 2023), because the remaining cash can come from loans or debt, which need to be paid back later with high interest.

Tangible Resources

In newspaper companies, employees and physical property are the two main tangible resources that hedge funds target for immediate profit returns (Coppins, 2021). Therefore, there two groups of variables, one is employee-related, which are: the total number of employees, the operational expense in wages and benefits, and the percentage of employee-related expenses out of the total operating expenses; another is physical property-related, which are: physical properties at cost value, the percentage of physical properties at cost value out of the total asset value, and land and buildings at cost value.

In terms of employee-related variables, there are two pieces of information directly addressed in the annual report: the total number of employees and the related operational expenses, such as wages and benefits (Kenton, 2020). To gain a comprehensive understanding of how this type of financial expense changes over an extended period, it is not sufficient to consider the changing trend individually, but also necessary to examine the percentage of it in relation to the total amount of operating expenses.

In terms of physical properties, the information is directly addressed by their cost value within a broad category of asset value in an annual report (Kenton, 2020). Similar to employee expenses, it is necessary to consider not only the individual trend changes but also how they have changed within the category to which they belong—total asset value. Additionally, the category of physical properties remains somewhat broad compared to what hedge funds target. This means that, in addition to buildings and land, which hedge funds are interested in, it also includes items like office equipment, furniture, and machinery (Kenton, 2020). In an annual report, the cost of buildings and land is also addressed individually, so it can be retrieved and analyzed separately.

The term "physical property at cost" in an annual report refers to the original cost at which the company purchased the property, and it does not reflect the current market value or the cost to replace the property at the present time (Twin, 2021). It's important to note that the original cost is typically lower than the replacement cost, especially when considering factors such as inflation rate and market development (Twin, 2021). Therefore, the original cost of physical property may not accurately reflect its true market value that hedge funds could potentially obtain through a sell-off, but it can still provide some economic context and information about the company's historical expenses in its physical assets.

Corporate Transactions: Spin-off, Merging, Bankruptcy

Hedge funds attempt to take advantage of opportunities created by significant transactional events of public companies, such as spin-offs, mergers/acquisitions, and bankruptcies, which make the companies the most vulnerable (Stulz, 2007). During the period when these transactional events occur, there are more than the usual negative effects that may happen (Chen, 2022).

Specifically, in terms of "spin-offs," the major negative impact that can make the company vulnerable is due to the parent company shareholders selling their spin-off shares, which causes the stock price to lose value for a period of time and also contributes to additional corporate debt (Depersio, 2022). Concerning "mergers/acquisitions," the acquiring company's share price tends to drop because it often pays a premium for the target company or incurs debt to finance the acquisition (Bloomenthal, 2022). As for "bankruptcy," it is the worst corporate transaction for shareholders; when a company files for bankruptcy protection, chances are its shares will lose value significantly, and the company will be delisted from its exchange (Phung, 2021). The public companies have less ability to resist another significant attack from outside when these extreme corporate transaction activities occur.

Public companies are required to list all strategy changes that occurred during the year in item 1 of the annual report, including significant corporate transactions. They also provide explanations and discuss concerns related to these transactions in item 2, which covers all potential negative effects or so-called risk factors. The section of risk factors in an annual report refers to problems or conflicts that could potentially impede corporate transactions (Wheelen, et al., 2017).

Annual Report Operational Measurement and Coding

Overall, the variables of P/E ratio, free cash flow, and tangible resources are related to number-based data collection, while the variable of corporate transactions involves thematic data collection.

P/E ratio (RQ1): As introduced earlier, although there is related information in annual reports, no specific value of P/E ratio is provided there. The most authoritative value of P/E ratio can be found on Yahoo Finance. The P/E ratio can never be a negative number; it is either a positive value or zero. This is because although earnings per share can be negative (meaning a public company is earning negatively), the calculation of the P/E ratio becomes meaningless, resulting in zero. This indicates that the company has lost money in that time period, and investing is not recommended.

Free cash flow (RQ2): There is a specific table labeled as 'free cash flow' in the financial statement item in an annual report (Fernando, 2025). This table details the operational incomes and expenditures, as well as any capital expenditures and financial investment. Usually, capital expenditures or financial investments lead to more dramatic changes in free cash flow, such as through debt or loans. The economic performance of operational income (i.e., advertising and circulation) is typically more gradual in a developed industry. The dedicated section on free cash flow is item 8 in an annual report.

Tangible resources (RQ3): There are two groups of variables that need to be measured: employee-related (RQ3-A) and physical property-related (RQ3-B). Regarding employee-related variables, there is a subsection about the total number of employees (RQ3-A-1), which can be directly found in the business review section—item 1. The expenses for employee wages and benefits (RQ3-A-2) are specified in the financial statement table of operational expenses—item 8. However, the percentage of employee-related expenses out of the total operational expenses (RQ3-A-3) needs to be calculated. As for physical property-related variables, the data regarding its value at cost (RQ3-B-1) can be directly coded from the financial statement table of asset value at cost—item 8. The percentage of physical property value out of the total asset value (RQ3-B-2) also needs to be calculated. Furthermore, specific data about the value at cost for land and buildings (RQ3-B-3) can be coded from an appendix table detailing the value of physical properties at cost.

Corporate transaction strategies (RQ4): There are three themes that should be specifically measured: spin-offs (RQ4-A), mergers (RQ4-B), and bankruptcies (RQ4-C). The related data need to be collected from two sections—Business Overview (item 1) and Risk Factors (item 1A). Moreover, if a corporate transaction strategy is only addressed in the "Business Overview" section of annual report and not highlighted in the "Risk Factors" section, it usually indicates that the company has confidence in its ability to control the impacts of the transaction. However, if the transaction is addressed and detailed in both the "Business Overview" section and the "Risk Factors" section, it usually shows that the company recognizes the likelihood of unpredictable and uncontrollable impacts, often indicating negative outcomes.

For operationalization, the logic is that all corporate transaction activities are required to be addressed in the section of Business Overview, but not all of them need to be addressed in the section of Risk Factors. If the company mentioned one of these three transaction activities—spin-offs (RQ4-A), mergers (RQ4-B), and bankruptcies (RQ4-C)—in the Business Overview section, a certain variable can be labeled as "B-Y." Otherwise, it is labeled as "B-N." If the company also mentioned the following information in the Risk Factors section, the variable of corporate transaction strategies can be labeled as "R-Y." Otherwise, it is labeled as "R-N." Only when a certain corporate strategy is labeled with both "B-Y" and "R-Y" can it be determined that there is a signal that might trigger hedge funds to take active action.

Study Two Measures—In-depth Interviews

The purpose in this study primarily focused on how hedge fund ownership impacts the newspaper industry through analyzing news management tasks, especially the conflict that is created by hedge fund's aggressive financial motives against the motives and professional values of news management. Specifically, management tasks in a knowledge industry include aligning with the owners' mission, setting operational objectives with rank-and-file employees, and maintaining social impacts (Drucker, 2008).

In this study, semi-structured interviews were conducted using a predetermined interview protocol. These interviews will offer an opportunity for participants to express and elaborate on their views, allowing for the collection of rich and detailed data (Denzin & Lincoln, 2008). In-depth interviews are well-suited for studies that involve purposive sampling of small, non-generalizable populations, wherein the interviewees are regarded as informants rather than simply respondents (Yin, 2012, p. 107).

Doing in-depth interviews involves gaining insights from the participants' perspectives and understanding their perceptions and experiences in depth (Lindlof & Taylor, 2017). This research method enables participants to articulate the intricacies and nuances of their perspectives (Denzin & Lincoln, 2008; Hawkins & Tull, 1994). The qualified participants for this study are news managers currently employed by daily newspapers that are owned by hedge funds, which are Tribune Publishing and McClatchy. Thus, their perspectives are highly meaningful for understanding the impacts of hedge fund ownership on the future of the daily newspaper industry.

Sampling

This study was also based on the data provided in their annual reports, but specifically from the latest ones they generated, as the qualified participants should be those currently employed. For Tribune Publishing, 2020 is the most recent report, while for McClatchy, the last annual report was produced in 2018. However, Tribune Publishing only provides detailed information for their flagship daily newspapers, totaling 11, while McClatchy lists all of theirs, which amounts to 30 daily newspapers in total.

Tribune Publishing (11 flagship daily newspapers, as of 2020):

Chicago Tribune (IL), *The Baltimore Sun* (MD), *The Capital Gazette* (MD), *Carroll County Times* (MD), *The Mercury News* (CA), *Hartford Courant* (CT), *Sun Sentinel* (FL), *Orlando Sentinel* (FL), *Daily Press* (VA), *The Virginian-Pilot* (VA), *The Morning Call* (PA).

McClatchy (30 daily newspapers in total, as of 2018)

Miami Herald (FL), *The Kansas City Star* (MO), *Star-Telegram* (TX), *The Charlotte Observer* (NC), *The Sacramento Bee* (CA), *The News & Observer* (NC), *The State* (SC), *El Nuevo Herald* (FL), *Lexington Herald-Leader* (KY), *The News Tribune* (WA), *The Wichita Eagle* (KS), *The Fresno Bee* (CA), *Idaho Statesman* (ID), *The Modesto Bee* (CA), *Belleville News-Democrat* (IL), *The Tribune* (CA), *The Telegraph* (GA), *The Island Packet* (SC), *The Herald* (SC), *Tri-City Herald* (WA), *The*

Bradenton Herald (FL), *Ledger-Enquirer* (GA), *Sun Herald* (MS), *The Sun News* (SC), *Centre Daily Times* (PA), *The Bellingham Herald* (WA), *The Olympian* (WA), *Merced Sun-Star* (CA), *The Herald-Sun* (NC), *The Beaufort Gazette* (SC).

In addition to these lists, for verifying the existence of these papers during recent years when the company did not generate annual reports, it is necessary to visit the websites of these newspapers individually to check the current situation. For example, Tribune Publishing cut the *Capital Gazette* (MD) in 2021 permanently (Benderev, 2021).

Moreover, there is no detailed employee or leadership information per daily newspaper that is provided in newspaper company's annual reports, so it is necessary to collect the concurrent related information from their websites. These newspapers usually address different job responsibilities by using different titles, such as the management track in editorial-based or business-based roles. For example, editorial-based management titles include the chief editor, managing editor, and sometimes senior editors, who oversee significant content areas. For smaller newspapers within the same newspaper company, some individuals may have dual responsibilities within both content and business areas. For example, in McClatchy, *The State* (SC), *The Island Packet* (SC), and *The Sun News* (SC), these three newspapers share the same Chief Editor/President.

Furthermore, the snowball sampling method was applied in this study. Snowball sampling involves recruiting participants who, in turn, help identify other potential subjects (Naderifar, Goli, & Ghaljaie, 2017). It can be an effective method for studying individuals facing particular circumstances that would otherwise pose challenges in reaching them (Naderifar, Goli, & Ghaljaie, 2017). One reason for using this method in the study is to target high-level management, who often have busy schedules and may not readily respond to unfamiliar email addresses. Another reason is that making any comments about their current hedge fund owners may not be appropriate given their position and the sensitivity of the situation. Lastly, due to the uncertainty surrounding potential layoffs, buyouts, and negotiations with new owners, openly expressing opinions may not be conducive to their job security. Therefore, snowball sampling offers a viable alternative recruiting method with direct email contact.

In short, because the purpose of this study is to examine how hedge fund ownership impacts the newspaper industry, with an emphasis on editorial-based management, the study focused on individuals who hold editorial-based leadership positions, regardless of whether they have other responsibilities or oversee multiple newspapers, and the possible titles focused on the range from editor/executive editor down to managing editor/assistant managing editor. Senior or investigative reporters who also shoulder significant responsibilities within the newsroom were also included as possible interviewees because of their level of knowledge of newsroom operations

Virtual interviews via Zoom were conducted in this study due to the national or regional nature of public newspaper companies (García-Avilés, 2021). This ensured that managers, located in various locations across the country, can be easily reached virtually. Each interview lasted from 40 to 60 minutes to allow for sufficient depth of comments and coverage of the entire interview protocol.

In-depth Interview Variables

Owners' missions

According to the literature review, two ownership missions deserve attention when news managers engage in day-to-day management of the newsroom: journalism quality and profit-driven motivation (Demers, 1996). In newspapers with public ownership, both these missions are taken into consideration due to the belief that high-quality journalism content can retain an appropriate audience size, consequently keeping advertisers engaged as well, which leads to the same goal of profit. However, if a hedge fund takes full control of a newspaper, not only will this ownership potentially eliminate the mission of journalism quality, but the concept of profit-driven motivation can differ from that upheld by public newspaper ownership. Unlike public newspaper ownership, motivated primarily by long-term profitability and limited tangible resources provided (Demers, 1996), the profit-driven approach under hedge fund ownership often prioritizes immediate cash gains. This is achieved by cutting tangible resources through large-scale layoffs (employee) and selling off physical properties (land and buildings) (Stulz, 2007). Eventually, hedge funds' immediate profit-driven motivation can curtail the newspaper's developmental opportunities.

Operational Objectives

According to the literature review, the economic environment became challenging around 2000 with the impact of the Internet. It further suffered as advertisers shifted toward digital products around and after the 2008 recession, alongside the development of social media (Picard, 2010). This tough competitive environment led to a dramatic drop in profitability for many newspapers, prompting the implementation of aggressive cost control strategies over the past decade (Pristin, 2013). The scarcity of available tangible resources has thus put news management's operational objectives in jeopardy, which is primarily manifested in a couple of aspects: the lack of training for young journalists (Escobar, 2018), and unfriendly working environment (Escobar, 2018; Killebrew, 2003).

Maintaining Social Impacts

In terms of maintaining social impacts, this variable category aims to capture insights about the threats that hedge fund ownership might pose to the newspaper industry and the implication for journalism in a democratic society. There are three related concepts that need to be addressed in this category: journalism professional values, public interest, and social responsibilities, which are all value-based issues.

Specifically, the variable of "Journalism professionalism values" will focus on reporting or publishing quality, as well as ethical issues because high ethical standards are highly valuable for professional journalists (Siebert et al., 1963). The variable of "Public interest" will focus on the newsroom impact, which will be oriented toward local community service, emphasizing the maintenance of connections with local issues and events (Merrill, 1974, 2012), such as cultivating news sources from the local council and local school district. The variable of "Social Responsibility" in this study will specifically focus on the societal impact, which includes the general insights about the implication for journalism in a democratic society (Siebert et al., 1963).

In-depth Interview Operational Measurement and Coding

The unit of analysis was the in-depth interviews with news managers. All in-depth interviews were conducted using the same semi-structured protocol. They were conducted remotely via Zoom, and transcriptions were recorded thereafter. The interviewees' words, phrases, or sentences were coded within the same categories of variables.

Owner's missions (RQ5): Two approaches of missions will be measured and coded in this category: journalism quality (RQ5-A) and profit-driven motivation (RQ5-B). For each mission, the interview protocol elicited perspectives from news managers about hedge fund ownership. Therefore, the protocol and coding process focused on the mission that the hedge fund owners is aiming to achieve, instead of whether the news managers support or resist. A couple of example interview questions are: "How does your current owner communicate journalistic quality to the newsroom?" and "How does your current owner communicate profit-driven motivation to the newsroom?."

Moreover, in order to achieve more detailed and specific information about the impacts of hedge fund ownership on the newsroom routine work, participants were asked to describe the process and evaluation procedures. A couple of example interview questions are: "Describe the owner's process, if any, for evaluating performance in journalism quality," and "Describe the owner's process, if any, for evaluating performance in profit-driven motivation."

Operational objectives (RQ6): Two approaches were also measured and coded: young journalists training (RQ6-A) and how to allocate overwhelming workload (RQ6-B). This set of protocol and coding process aims to examine how news managers effectively manage rank-and-file journalists by establishing clear objectives.

However, tangible resources (i.e., employee and physical property) are crucial scholarly concepts for news managers to effectively implement operational objectives (Picard & Van Weezel, 2008). Therefore, the participants were first asked to briefly share their perspectives on the impacts of hedge fund ownership on tangible resources. For example, questions included: "How have the layoffs and buyouts led by your current owner affected your daily newsroom management?" and "How far is your newsroom located from the primary local news sources? Does this pose challenges for your journalists in their news collection work?" Additionally, participants were asked about the impacts on their day-to-day journalism job performance, such as "How has the leadership of your current owner impacted news coverage or news beats?"

When the interview questions relate to young journalists' training (RQ6-A) and overwhelming workload (RQ6-B), the aim is to examine through the lens of tangible resources. For example, questions included: "What approach do you use to engage senior journalists in mentoring newer ones?" and "What different print and digital media platforms does your team need to maintain, including social media platforms?"

Maintaining social impacts (RQ7): three related concepts with different focuses were measured and coded: journalism professional values (RQ7-A), public interest (RQ7-B), and social responsibilities (RQ7-C). Given that journalism professional values relate to the journalists' daily work, specifically focusing on reporting quality with ethical standards, the protocol and coding process emphasized key concepts such as "news judgment," "reporting autonomy," and "ethical codes." Considering that public interest relates to the newsroom community impact, the protocol and coding process will focus on key concepts such as "local news sources" and "community connections." Finally, in terms of the notion that social responsibilities pertain to the implementation of journalism for a democratic society, the protocol and coding process concentrated on key concepts such as "democracy," "journalism function," and "social responsibilities."

Additionally, for qualitative research data analysis, coding is a crucial analysis technique. Coding methods involve processes that reveal themes embedded in the interview data and enable the collected data to be assembled, categorized, and thematically sorted (Williams & Moser, 2019). Specifically, twenty questions were asked to the participants one by one, ensuring that the transcripts of each interview followed the same order. Once all interview transcripts were ready, the feedback from all participants was reorganized according to different research questions. This method consolidates all relevant data into one file for each research question, making it easier for coding and preventing the loss of important information.

Specifically, regarding the in-depth interviews where participants have more freedom to express their perspectives, there were instances where they overlapped questions or condensed similar ideas. First, the researcher needed to ensure that all questions were answered. Second, some participants provided excessive information for earlier questions, resulting in fewer new insights for subsequent questions. In such cases, the researcher had to prompt them again when moving to the next question to ensure no points were missed. Additionally, some participants provided brief feedback, prompting the researcher to ask follow-up questions to encourage them to provide more detailed information. These steps can help categorize the final data thematically and efficiently. During the process of analyzing the data, regarding certain variables, participants' perspectives were categorized together, marking their different insights or detailed information. For example, concerning the variable of young journalist training, some participants directly mentioned the lack of official mentoring, while others extended this idea to include high turnover rates and poor job contracts for new hires. All of this information was beneficial to this variable and even inspired more ideas for future studies.

References

Benderev, C. (2021, March). Capital Gazette: "We Are The Newsroom." NPR. https://www.npr.org/2021/03/10/975601926/capital-gazette-we-are-the-newsroom

Bloomenthal, A. (2022, June). How company stocks move during an acquisition. *Investopedia*. https://www.investopedia.com/ask/answers/203.asp#:~:text=Key%20Takeaways,debt%20to%20finance%20the%20acquisition

Brav, A., Jiang, W., & Kim, H. (2015). Recent advances in research on hedge fund activism: Value creation and identification. *Annual Review of Financial Economics, 7*, 579–595.

Caruana, F. J., Roman, M., Hernández-Sánchez, J., & Solli, P. (2015). Longitudinal studies. *Journal of Thoracic Disease, 7*(11), E537.

Chen, J. (2022, July). What is the stock market? *Investopedia*. https://www.investopedia.com/terms/s/stockmarket.asp

Chyi, H. I., & Tenenboim, O. (2019). Charging more and wondering why readership declined? A longitudinal study of US newspapers' price hikes, 2008–2016. *Journalism Studies, 20*(14), 2113–2129.

Coppins, M. (2021, October). A secretive hedge fund is gutting newsrooms. *The Atlantic*. https://www.theatlantic.com/magazine/archive/2021/11/alden-global-capital-killing-americas-newspapers/620171/

Demers, D. (1996). Corporate newspaper structure, editorial page vigor, and social change. *Journalism & Mass Communication Quarterly, 73*(4), 857–877.

Denzin, N. K., & Lincoln, Y. S. (2008). Introduction: The discipline and practice of qualitative research.

Depersio, G. (2022, April). How do spinoffs impact investors in parent and subsidiary companies? *Investopedia*. https://www.investopedia.com/ask/answers/032415/how-do-spinoffs-impact-investors-both-parent-and-subsidiary-companies.asp#:~:text=The%20sum%20of%20the%20two,shareholders%20selling%20their%20spinoff%20shares

Drucker, P. (2008). Introduction: Management and managers defined; management as a social function and liberal art; knowledge is all. *Management*, 1–25.

Escobar, N. (2018, February). How do young journalists get their training? *ProPublica*. https://www.propublica.org/article/ask-ppil-how-do-young-journalists-get-their-training

Fernando, J. (2023, July). Free Cash Flow (FCF): Formula to calculate and interpret it. *Investopedia*. https://www.investopedia.com/terms/f/freecashflow.asp

Fernando, J (2025). Free Cash Flow (FCF): How to Calculate and Interpret It. *Investopedia*. Retrieved from: https://www.investopedia.com/terms/f/freecashflow.asp

Gannett Annual Report. (2015). *Gannett*. Retrieved from: https://www.annualreports.com/HostedData/AnnualReportArchive/g/NYSE_GCI_2015.pdf

Gannett Annual Report. (2022). *Gannett*. Retrieved from: https://s202.q4cdn.com/162862548/files/doc_financials/2022/ar/2022-annual-report.pdf

García-Avilés, J. A. (2021). Journalism as usual? Managing disruption in virtual newsrooms during the COVID-19 crisis. *Digital Journalism, 9*(9), 1239–1260.

Hall, K. (2020, August). Bankruptcy judge approves the sale of McClatchy to hedge fund Chatham Asset Management. *McClatchy*. https://www.mcclatchydc.com/news/nation-world/national/article244710217.html

Hawkins, D. I., & Tull, D. S. (1994). *Essentials of marketing research*. Macmillan Publishing Company.

Hayes, A. (2023, June). Annual report explained: How to read and write them. *Investopedia*. https://www.investopedia.com/terms/a/annualreport.asp

Kenton, W. (2020, March). 10-K. *Investopedia*. https://www.investopedia.com/terms/1/10-k.asp

Killebrew, K. C. (2003). Culture, creativity and convergence: Managing journalists in a changing information workplace. *International Journal on Media Management, 5*(1), 39–46.

Lee, E. (2019, July). Under hedge fund set to own McClatchy, Canadian newspapers endured big cuts. *The New York Times*. https://www.nytimes.com/2020/07/16/business/media/hedge-fund-chatham-mcclatchy-postmedia-newspapers.html

Lee Enterprises Annual Report. (2022). *Lee Enterprises*. Retrieved from: https://investors.lee.net/staticfiles/c82f89e9-ce07-41a1-b8dd-3898ff82e831

Lindlof, T. R., & Taylor, B. C. (2017). *Qualitative communication research methods*. Sage Publications.

Mansouri, K. (2022, November). Hedge fund's takeover of Lee Enterprises ends as investors brace for advertising decline. *NPR*. https://news.stlpublicradio.org/economy-business/2022-11-15/hedge-funds-takeover-of-lee-enterprises-ends-as-investors-brace-for-advertising-decline

Martin, H. J. (1998). Measuring newspaper profits: Developing a standard of comparison. *Journalism & Mass Communication Quarterly, 75*(3), 500–517.

McClatchy Company Records. (n.d.). *Online archive of California*. https://oac.cdlib.org/findaid/ark:/13030/kt4p3025zf/admin/

McClatchy Annual Report. (2019). *McClathcy*. Retrieved from: https://www.sec.gov/Archives/edgar/data/1056087/000105608720000014/mni-20191229x10k.htm

Merrill, J. C. (1974). *The imperative of freedom: A philosophy of journalistic autonomy*.

Merrill, J. C. (2012). Journalism and democracy. In *Changing the News* (pp. 45–62). Routledge.

Morgenson, G., & Rosner, J. (2023). *These are the plunderers: How private equity runs – And Wrecks – America*. Simon and Schuster.

Mullin, B. (2021, November). Lee enterprises enacts poison pill to guard against Alden takeover. *The Wall Street Journal*. https://www.wsj.com/articles/lee-enterprises-enacts-poison-pill-to-guard-against-alden-takeover-11637793121

Murphy, C. (2023, May). Using the price to earnings ratio and PEG to assess a stock. *Investopedia*.

Naderifar, M., Goli, H., & Ghaljaie, F. (2017). Snowball sampling: A purposeful method of sampling in qualitative research. *Strides in Development of Medical Education, 14*(3).

Phung, A. (2021, October). What happens to stocks after Chapter 11? *Investopedia*. https://www.investopedia.com/ask/answers/06/chapter11stocksbonds.asp

Picard, R. G. (2010). The future of the news industry. *Media and Society, 5*, 365–379.

Picard, R. G. (2011). *The economics and financing of media companies*. Fordham University Press.

Picard, R. G., & Van Weezel, A. (2008). Capital and control: Consequences of different forms of newspaper ownership. *The International Journal on Media Management, 10*(1), 22–31.

Pristin, T. (2013, October). Struggling newspapers sell off old headquarters. *The New York Times*. https://www.nytimes.com/2013/10/23/realestate/commercial/struggling-newspapers-sell-off-old-headquarters.html

Reuters. (2011). Newspaper group Lee Enterprises files for bankruptcy. *Reuters*. Retrieved from: https://www.reuters.com/article/2011/12/12/us-leeenterprises-idUSTRE7BB26I20111212/

Riffe, D., Lacy, S., Fico, F., & Watson, B. (2019). *Analyzing media messages: Using quantitative content analysis in research*. Routledge.

SEC.gov. (n.d.). How to read a 10-K/10-Q. *U.S. Securities and exchange commission*. https://www.sec.gov/fast-answers/answersreada10khtm.html

Siebert, F., Peterson, T., & Schramm, W. (1963). *Four theories of the press: The authoritarian, libertarian, social responsibility, and Soviet communist concepts of what the press should be and do.* University of Illinois press.

Snider, M. (2020, January). Warren Buffett and Berkshire Hathaway to sell its newspapers to Lee Enterprises for $140 million. *USA Today.* https://www.usatoday.com/story/money/2020/01/29/warren-buffett-newspapers-berkshire-hathaway-lee-enterprises-newspapers/4607530002/

Stulz, R. M. (2007). Hedge funds: Past, present, and future. *Journal of Economic Perspectives, 21*(2), 175–194.

Tribune Publishing Annual Report. (2020). *Tribune Publishing.* Retrieved from: https://www.annualreports.com/HostedData/AnnualReports/PDF/NYSE_TPUB_2020.pdf

Tribune Publishing Annual Report. (2021). *Tribune Publishing.* Retrieved from: https://annualreport.stocklight.com/NASDAQ/TPCO/21854715.pdf

Twin, A. (2021, April). What is replacement cost and how does it work? *Investopedia.* https://www.investopedia.com/terms/r/replacementcost.asp

Wagner, H. (2022, July). Free cash flow yield: The best fundamental indicator. *Investopedia.* https://www.investopedia.com/articles/fundamental-analysis/09/free-cash-flow-yield.asp

Wheelen, T. L., Hunger, J. D., Hoffman, A. N., & Bamford, C. E. (2017). Strategic management and business policy (p. 55).

Williams, M., & Moser, T. (2019). The art of coding and thematic exploration in qualitative research. *International Management Review, 15*(1), 45–55.

Yin, R. K. (2012). *Case study methods* (p. 107).

Zucchi, K. (2022). Tracking your portfolio on Yahoo! Finance. *Investopedia.* https://www.investopedia.com/articles/investing/092214/tracking-your-portfolio-yahoo-finance.asp\

6

Study One: Results and Discussion
Factors That Attract Hedge Funds to Harvest the U.S. Newspaper Industry

Abstract Most importantly, this recorded data provides insights into how they were all highly vulnerable to external hostile attacks, encompassing the unstable P/E ratio, negative or dramatically changing free cash flow, insufficient tangible resources, and emerging corporate transactions.

Keywords P/E ratios • Free cash flow • Tangible resources • Operational revenue • Physical resource cues

In all, this research analyzed data from four newspaper companies over a span of 16 years (2007–2022), totaling 55 annual reports, including 16 from Gannett, 16 from Lee, 9 from Tribune Publishing, and 14 from McClatchy.

Gannett and Lee Enterprises consistently published annual reports each year, resulting in 16 reports per company. Tribune Publishing became an independent publicly traded company in 2013 after spinning off from its parent company and focusing on the news publishing business. It began providing annual reports in 2014, including data from 2013. However, their 2016 annual report was inaccessible to the public for unknown reasons, but the relevant data for this study can be found in the subsequent annual reports. They ultimately ceased publishing formal annual reports in 2021 after the acquisition by Alden hedge fund was completed. Thus, this research included a total of 9 annual reports from Tribune Publishing. In the case of McClatchy, they faced bankruptcy and filed for Chapter 11 in 2008 to 2009. Consequently, they were unable to sell stocks and provide annual reports during that period. However, they were permitted to continue operations, which means some information can still be found in their 2010 annual report, such as detailed operating revenue in 2008 and 2009. Additionally, McClatchy's annual report in 2012 is not accessible to the public for unknown reasons, but the related information for this study is available in subsequent annual reports. In 2020, it transitioned from being publicly traded to privately owned by hedge funds. As a result, a total of 14 annual reports from McClatchy were analyzed in this research.

Although these four companies have all experienced attacks from hedge funds, Tribune Publishing and McClatchy are already owned by hedge funds, with the acquisitions completed, while Gannett and Lee still maintain their independence. Therefore, in the data analysis, the data will be grouped by hedge fund-owned newspaper companies and publicly owned newspaper companies that faced hostile attacks, in order to clearly narrate the findings.

Overall, the data collected from these four newspaper companies can all corroborate the declining economic performance of the U.S. newspaper industry in the past decade, an idea explored in the literature review, as demonstrated through their operating revenue.

In terms of **operating revenue** (Table 6.1), all observed newspaper companies experienced a dramatic decrease, each with varying rates. For example, Lee exhibited the best performance in operating revenue, but it still declined by 30% from $1 billion in 2007 to $800 million in 2022. McClatchy experienced the steepest decline, dropping by 69% from $2 billion in 2007 to $700 million in 2019. Tribune Publishing experienced a drop of 58% from $1.8 billion in 2013 to $750 million in 2020. Although Gannett also saw a significant decline of 57% from $7 billion in 2007 to $3 billion in 2022, it is the only one that halted the declining trend and experienced a noticeable rise starting in 2020 and 2021.

Table 6.1 Change in operating revenue in observed period

Year	Gannett	Lee Enterprises	Tribune Publishing	McClatchy
2007	$7,439,460	$1,120,194	–	$2,260,363
2008	$6,767,650	$1,028,868	–	$1,900,456
2009	$5,509,603	$842,030	–	$1,471,584
2010	$5,438,678	$780,648	–	$1,375,232
2011	$5,239,989	$756,104	–	$1,351,854
2012	$5,353,197	$710,486	–	$1,309,639
2013	$5,161,362	$674,740	$1,795,107	$1,242,237
2014	$3,171,878	$656,697	$1,707,978	$1,146,552
2015	$2,885,012	$648,543	$1,672,820	$1,056,574
2016	$3,047,474	$614,364	$1,606,378	$977,093
2017	$3,146,480	$566,943	$1,524,018	$903,592
2018	$2,916,838	$543,955	$1,005,662	$807,226
2019	$1,867,909	$509,854	$945,777	$709,516
2020	$3,405,670	$618,004	$746,250	–
2021	$3,208,083	$794,649	–	–
2022	$2,945,303	$780,969	–	–

The term of Operating Revenue includes Advertising, Circulation, Marketing, and other
$ in thousand

Gannett's operating revenue increased significantly by 89% from $1.8 billion in 2019 to $3.4 billion. However, it has since slightly decreased to $3.2 billion in 2021 (-6%) and to $2.9 billion in 2022 (-1%).

In addition, among the publicly owned newspaper companies that faced hostile attacks, Gannett and Lee either exhibited better operating revenue performance or demonstrated an ability to adjust and improve their operating income. In contrast, the hedge fund-owned newspaper companies, Tribune Publishing and McClatchy, experienced a significant drop in operational revenue with no signs of rebounding.

RQ1—P/E Ratio (Table 6.2)

In most of the recent decade, these four newspaper companies all exhibited low P/E ratios, indicating a lack of confidence in the stock market in their future profit-generating abilities. Among the four newspaper companies, the best-performing one is Lee Enterprises, which achieved

Table 6.2 Changes in P/E ratios in observed period

Year	Gannett	Lee Enterprises	Tribune Publishing	McClatchy
2009	0.00	0.00	–	5.80
2010	0.00	2.96	–	10.86
2011	0.00	0.00	–	3.79
2012	0.00	0.00	–	0.00
2013	0.00	0.00	–	15.45
2014	0.00	40.89	11.22	0.78
2015	0.00	3.65	13.74	0.00
2016	0.00	4.46	0.00	0.00
2017	0.00	2.58	82.02	0.00
2018	0.00	5.70	1.74	0.00
2019	0.00	8.82	0.00	0.00
2020	0.00	9.55	0.00	–
2021	0.00	5.51	–	–
2022	0.00	0.00	–	–

positive ratios in 9 out of 12 years and reached its peak in 2014 (P/E = 40.89). Tribune Publishing had positive P/E ratios for two years after re-entering the stock market in 2014, reaching its historical peak in 2017 (P/E ratio = 82.02), but subsequently declined to zero. McClatchy also achieved positive P/E ratios in five out of 12 years. In contrast, Gannett performed most poorly among these four companies, with a P/E ratio of 0 for all 12 years.

In addition, Gannett and Lee, the publicly owned newspaper companies that experienced hostile attacks from hedge funds, either have more years with a positive P/E ratio (Lee) or consistently maintain the lowest P/E ratio, thereby remaining outside the attention of investors (Gannett). Meanwhile, Tribune Publishing and McClatchy, the hedge fund-owned newspaper companies, both surprised the stock market significantly, experiencing periods of high anticipation and dramatic losses of confidence, with P/E ratios bouncing between zero and 82.02 (Tribune Publishing) or between zero and 15.45 (McClatchy).

RQ2—Free Cash Flow (Table 6.3)

All four observed newspaper companies' free cash flow records had shown a mix of positive and negative cash flows, often fluctuating above and below the breakeven line ($0). Specifically, Gannett reached its peak positive free cash flow in 2013 ($300 million) and its lowest point in 2016 (-$80 million). The data indicates that in years with more positive free cash flow (e.g., 2010, 2015, 2019), the absolute values are higher than in years with more negative free cash flow (e.g., 2018, 2021, 2022). Lee demonstrated a more stable performance along the breakeven line, not experiencing significant highs or lows in its free cash flow during the 16-year period compared to other newspaper companies. Furthermore, Tribune Publishing and McClatchy sustained negative performance for several consecutive years. Tribune Publishing, for instance, recorded negative free cash flows for three consecutive years (2017, 2018, 2019), while McClatchy recorded negative figures in 2015–2016 and 2018–2019.

A notable fact emerged: publicly owned newspaper companies that successfully repelled hedge funds' attacks (such as Gannett and Lee) have

Table 6.3 Change in free cash flow in observed period

Year	Gannett	Lee Enterprises	Tribune Publishing	McClatchy
2007	–($17,007)	–($8638)	–	$6235
2008	$21,700	$23,459	–	–($20,818)
2009	–($154)	–($15,554)	–	$1159
2010	$84,219	$11,517	–	$11,351
2011	–($16,088)	$4133	–	$68,512
2012	$8104	–($9635)	–	$140,050
2013	$294,173	$3642	–($4074)	–($32,277)
2014	–($6649)	–($858)	$26,981	$140,050
2015	$124,749	–($5570)	$4157	–($211,529)
2016	–($82,372)	$5850	$157,517	–($4041)
2017	$5820	–($6363)	–($8696)	$94,096
2018	–($27,171)	–($5241)	–($53,936)	–($80,799)
2019	$135,894	$3265	–($39,285)	–($13,392)
2020	$18,062	$25,088	$36,657	–
2021	–($63,107)	–($7621)	–	–
2022	–($38,815)	–($9927)	–	–

$ in thousand

stronger financial management capabilities, enabling them to access more cash sources. In contrast, the two companies currently owned by hedge funds had limited capabilities prior to the hedge fund attacks.

RQ3—Tangible Resources (Employee and Physical Property)

This research question category includes two groups of variables: those related to employees and those related to physical property. These variables are analyzed over a span of 16 years. Specifically, there are six tangible resource variables in this category in total, including three employee-related variables and three physical property-related variables. The three employee-related variables are: the number of employees, the expenses for employee wages and benefits, and the percentage of employee-related expenses out of the total operational expenses. As for the physical property-related variables, these variables are: the value at cost of physical property, the percentage of physical property value out of the total asset value, and the value at cost for land and buildings.

In terms of the three employee-related variables, the variable of **the number of employees** (Table 6.4) indicates that all four observed newspaper companies have experienced rounds of layoffs and reductions since 2007. McClatchy achieved the highest reduction rate in employee numbers, experiencing an 81% reduction from 2007 to 2019. Tribune Publishing experienced a 61% reduction in their employee numbers. Lee Enterprises had the lowest reduction, but still reached a total of 37%. Gannett underwent a significant round of layoffs, reducing their employee count by 40% in just one year—decreasing their employee numbers from 31,250 in 2014 to 18,700 in 2015, making an overall reduction of 76%.

In addition, no obvious pattern was found in terms of the reduction of employee numbers between the two groups: public newspaper companies that experienced hostile attacks from hedge funds (Gannett and Lee), and the hedge fund-owned newspaper companies (Tribune Publishing and McClatchy). Lee demonstrates a substantially lower reduction rate (37%), about half that of the other three companies. The

Table 6.4 Change in the number of employees in observed period

Year	Gannett	Lee Enterprises	Tribune Publishing	McClatchy
2007	46,100	6950	–	14,307
2008	41,500	6200	–	–
2009	35,000	5400	–	–
2010	32,600	5070	–	7773
2011	31,000	4600	–	6880
2012	30,700	4900	–	–
2013	31,600	3700	–	6630
2014	31,250	3500	7300	5780
2015	18,700	3300	7165	5100
2016	17,100	2914	–	4600
2017	15,300	2628	6581	3900
2018	13,700	2315	4448	3300
2019	21,255	2332	4114	2700
2020	18,100	4524	2865	–
2021	13,800	5130	–	–
2022	11,200	4365	–	–

The Term of Employee Number only includes full-time employees

other three companies all showed aggressive employee reductions from 2009 to 2022, including 61% (Tribune Publishing), 76% (Gannett), and 81% (McClatchy).

In terms of the three employee-related variables, particularly the variable of **employee-related expenses** (Table 6.5), all four newspaper companies have implemented significant cost control measures from 2007 to 2022. For example, McClatchy records showed a 72% decrease in employee expenses from 2007 to 2019 right before filing for bankruptcy. Tribune Publishing reduced its employee expenses by approximately half, a 49% reduction from 2007 to 2020 by the time being acquired by a hedge fund. The other two newspaper companies also experienced a steady decline in employee expenses over the 16-year period, with Gannett at 33% and Lee Enterprises at 28%.

In addition, the publicly owned newspaper companies that experienced hostile attacks from hedge funds (Gannett and Lee) demonstrated a steady decline in employee expenses, albeit less pronounced than the two hedge fund-owned newspaper companies did. Tribune Publishing and McClatchy, the hedge fund-owned newspaper companies, both

Table 6.5 Change in employee-related expenses contributed to the total operating expenses during the observed period

Year	Gannett	%	Lee Enterprises	%	Tribune Publishing	%	McClatchy	%
2007	$1,270,090	22%	$439,426	47%	–	–	$911,964	19%
2008	$1,277,962	9%	$421,652	21%	–	–	$822,771	47%
2009	$1,186,970	25%	$339,014	34%	–	–	$582,241	46%
2010	$1,187,633	27%	$315,698	46%	–	–	$519,179	46%
2011	$1,223,458	28%	$299,416	34%	–	–	$457,707	40%
2012	$1,303,427	29%	$276,379	45%	–	–	$443,401	39%
2013	$1,291,858	29%	$254,831	34%	$597,882	37%	$432,255	39%
2014	$765,465	26%	$243,054	44%	$596,366	37%	$411,881	39%
2015	$707,022	26%	$239,028	44%	$649,905	39%	$395,449	30%
2016	$795,548	27%	$229,752	44%	$597,293	38%	$383,673	40%
2017	$836,306	27%	$209,692	44%	$549,363	38%	$338,588	39%
2018	$808,468	28%	$196,334	42%	$441,558	42%	$298,033	36%
2019	$602,106	30%	$182,869	41%	$360,779	38%	$251,677	25%
2020	$999,789	26%	$243,023	43%	$303,027	37%	–	–
2021	$902,064	29%	$330,896	44%	–	–	–	–
2022	$852,488	29%	$317,789	42%	–	–	–	–

The Term of employee expense includes wages, benefits, and compensations
$ in thousand

reduced more than half of their expenses on employee-related costs, with McClatchy notably cutting 72% of its employee expenses.

In terms of the three employee-related variables, particularly the variable of **the percentage that employee-related expenses contribute to the total operating expense** (Table 6.5). Each company had maintained a relatively steady percentage of employee expenses out of the total expense during 2007 to 2022. For example, Gannett's percentage rose from 22% in 2007 to 29% in 2022, while McClatchy's rose from 19% in 2007 to 25% in 2019. Tribune Publishing maintained an unchanged percentage, remaining at 37% from 2007 to 2022. Lee showed a slight decrease, going from 47% in 2007 to 42% in 2022, albeit still relatively high.

Additionally, based on the data recorded from the two hedge fund-owned newspaper companies, at the time they were acquired by hedge funds, both were spending a significant portion on employees (Tribune Publishing was 37% in 2020 and McClatchy was 25% in 2019). This suggests that hedge funds can generate immediate savings by laying off employees at these companies. Notably, this explains why Lee and Gannett have become attractive targets, with recent spending percentages of 42% and 29%, respectively.

In terms of the three physical property-related variables, particularly the variable of the **physical property value at cost**, the collected data shows that the four observed newspaper companies all underwent significant cost control measures to varying degrees since 2007, with no signs of recovery until 2022 (Table 6.6). For example, Gannett experienced the largest decrease rate (-88%) from $2.6 billion to $0.3 billion over the 16 years, Lee decreased by -77%, Tribune Publishing by 70%, and McClatchy by 78%. Only McClatchy once showed a slight increase in 2012 with 0.01%, while the other three companies all experienced a steadfast decline in the cost control of physical properties during 2007 to 2022.

Table 6.6 Change in the cost value of physical property during the observed period, and the percentage out of the total assets value

Year	Gannett	%	Lee Enterprises	%	Tribune Publishing	%	McClatchy	%
2007	$2,615,670	16%	$324,655	10%	–		$942,092	23%
2008	$2,221,494	28%	$292,828	15%	–		–	
2009	$1,971,818	28%	$262,969	17%	–		$767,580	23%
2010	$1,758,111	26%	$235,400	16%	–		$709,208	23%
2011	$1,640,227	25%	$212,040	18%	–		$760,977	25%
2012	$1,518,678	24%	$185,219	17%	–		$733,729	24%
2013	$1,669,632	18%	$168,913	20%	–		$458,705	18%
2014	$934,483	39%	$157,371	19%	$148,575	22%	$404,238	16%
2015	$896,585	37%	$143,769	19%	$139,377	17%	$364,219	19%
2016	$1,087,701	38%	$128,562	19%	$66,836	8%	$297,506	16%
2017	$933,334	36%	$114,196	18%	$97,976	11%	$257,639	17%
2018	$796,009	32%	$92,328	16%	$132,629	18%	$233,692	18%
2019	$815,807	20%	$82,039	15%	$121,710	18%	$203,575	22%
2020	$590,272	19%	$105,609	12%	$46,459	8%	–	
2021	$415.384	0.01%	$83,266	10%	–		–	
2022	$305,994	13%	$73,713	10%	–		–	

The Term of Physical Property at cost includes Land, Building, Equipment
$ in thousand

In addition, the data demonstrated that all four observed newspaper companies had gone through a prolonged period of selling off their physical properties. This was likely done to a compensate for lost income, increase their revenues, and maintain their stock prices at higher and somewhat attractive levels for shareholders and normal investors.

In terms of the three physical property-related variables, particularly the variable of **the changing percentage that contributes to the total asset value**, all four newspaper companies have implemented value reduction from 2007 to 2022 (Table 6.6). According to the recorded data, Tribune Publishing experienced significant changes, decreasing from 24% to 9%. The other companies generally maintained similar percentages, with Gannett decreasing from 16% to 13%, Lee remaining at 10%, and McClatchy decreasing from 23% to 22% (2019).

However, Gannett and Tribune Publishing showed some erratic changes in the percentage of physical property out of the total. For instance, Gannett's percentage changed from 18% in 2013 to 39% in 2014, and remained at 32% until 2018, then sharply dropped to 20% before reaching 13% in 2022. Tribune Publishing also showed a significant change, but in the opposite way. They downsized their percentage of physical property out of the total from 22% in 2014 to 8% in 2016, rebounded to 20% in 2018, and then sharply drop to 9% in 2020 before being acquired by a hedge fund. Moreover, Lee and McClatchy have not shown dramatic changes over this span of 16 years.

In addition, when compared with the two groups—the publicly owned newspaper companies that experienced hostile attacks from hedge funds (Gannett and Lee) and the hedge fund-owned newspaper companies (Tribune Publishing and McClatchy)—no clear patterns the distinguish the two groups. However, there were some unusual changes during certain periods. For example, Tribune Publishing was consistently selling off properties from 2014 to 2016, but they began purchasing properties again by 2018 before experiencing a large sell-off in 2020. These changes might reflect their attempts to avoid external hostile takeovers.

In terms of the three physical property-related variables, particularly the variable of **the value at cost for land and buildings**, these four companies exhibited different performances (Table 6.7). An important point to note is that the value of land and buildings is calculated before total

Table 6.7 Change in the cost value of lands and buildings during the observed period

Year	Gannett	Lee Enterprises	Tribune Publishing	McClatchy
2007	$1,770,390	$222,391	–	$600,633
2008	$1,672,563	$226,888	–	–
2009	$1,630,087	$225,938	–	$585,721
2010	$1,539,147	$222,419	–	$588,243
2011	$1,515,945	$218,267	–	$670,580
2012	$1,413,808	$213,279	–	$676,910
2013	$1,477,273	$208,464	–	$453,951
2014	$867,548	$204,215	$6434	$426,810
2015	$836,908	$201,988	$7377	$418,223
2016	$1,007,751	$195,192	$13,388	$364,862
2017	$915,131	$192,562	$42,635	$326,065
2018	$766,494	$167,808	$82,399	$300,492
2019	$522,342	$165,493	$86,404	$273,617
2020	$423,140	$147,186	$42,361	–
2021	$287,803	$123,466	–	–
2022	$209,985	$109,616	–	–

$ in thousand

depreciation in the annual reports, while the value at cost for physical properties and the total value of assets are both calculated after factoring in total depreciation. As a result, there is no direct numerical connection between them. Gannett, as usual, implemented aggressive cost control measures, resulting in an 88% reduction from $1.7 billion to $200 million in 2022. Lee and McClatchy showed similar reduction rates: Lee decreased by 51% from $200 million in 2007 to $100 million in 2022, while McClatchy reduced by 54% from $600 million in 2007 to $300 million in 2019. However, Tribune Publishing displayed an incredible increase in the cost value of land and buildings, experiencing a 558% surge from $6 million in 2014 to $42 million in 2020.

In addition, no obvious pattern was found when comparing the two groups—the public newspaper companies that experienced hostile attacks from hedge funds (Gannett and Lee), and the hedge fund-owned newspaper companies (Tribune Publishing and McClatchy). Only Tribune Publishing exhibited significant differences compared to the others.

RQ4—Corporate Transactions (Table 6.8)

Overall, these four newspaper companies all underwent one or multiple extreme corporate transactions, including spin-offs, mergers, or bankruptcies, which were described in both the business overview and risk factors sections. For example, Gannett acquired Dallas News in 2012, and separated from their publishing business and became an individual company in 2015. Lee Enterprises acquired BH Media Group in 2020. It is worth noting that Lee Enterprises filed for bankruptcy in 2011 and 2012 but has since emerged from it. As for the former publicly traded newspaper companies, Tribune Publishing announced a spin-off plan from their parent media group in 2013, which was successfully

Table 6.8 Corporate transactions of spin-off, merge, and bankruptcy during the observed period

2007–2022	Spin-off	Merge	Bankruptcy
Gannett	• Gannett completes Spin-Off of publishing business in 2015	• Gannett bought DallasNews in 2013	
Lee Enterprises		• Lee Enterprises bought BH media group in 2020	• Lee Enterprises filed for bankruptcy in 2011–2012
Tribune Publishing	• Tribune Publishing completed Spin-Off in 2014		• Tribune Publishing filed for bankruptcy in 2008–2013 • Mr. Ferro sold his 25% stake in 2019
McClatchy	–	–	• McClatchy filed for bankruptcy in 2008–2009 • McClatchy filed for bankruptcy in 2020

completed in 2014. This spin-off was a strategy aimed at recovering from the bankruptcy the company faced from 2008 to 2013. McClatchy, on the other hand, experienced bankruptcy twice, first in 2008 and 2009 and then again in 2020. In addition, Gannett may be facing a substantial risk from indebtedness, specifically from a large long-term loan due in 2026 and 2027. On October 15, 2021, Gannett issued a 5-year term loan (Senior Notes) due on November 1, 2026, along with 6.0% Senior Secured Convertible Notes due in 2027, totaling a $1.045 billion loan due eventually. According to Gannett's 2022 annual report, these debt service obligations currently require them to maintain a minimum cash flow liquidity of $30 million at the end of each fiscal quarter. Failure to meet these obligations may restrict their operational abilities and render it impractical to pay dividends in the near future.

In all, if considering the timing of when hedge funds took action, it seems clear that many of the hostile actions were triggered by these corporate transactions. For example, Alden attacked Lee in 2020 while it was undergoing acquisition with BH Media group. A former executive board member of Tribune Publishing sold his 25% stake to Alden, which then triggered Alden to take over even more aggressively in the stock market for Tribune Publishing. Meanwhile, McClatchy began to file for bankruptcy in 2020, and Chatham Wealth Management stepped in. Even though there was no apparent catalyst for Alden's hostile attacks on Gannett in 2019, as indicated in its annual reports, Gannett sold off a lot of property during that year. This action could have been an attempt to fend off a takeover, as Gannett was able to raise enough money by selling properties to remain public.

Discussion

Overall, based on the analysis of annual reports for four public newspaper companies since 2007 to 2022, totaling 55 annual reports, it is evident that they all experienced a challenging economic situation, as reflected in their ongoing decline in operating revenue. Most importantly, this recorded data also provides insights into how they were all highly vulnerable to external hostile attacks. Specifically, all assumed factors influencing hedge funds' acquisition and harvesting actions have been examined, encompassing the unstable P/E ratio (RQ1), negative or dramatically changed free cash flow (RQ2), sufficient tangible resources (RQ3), and the emerging corporate transactions (RQ4). Moreover, some positive experiences have also been observed among the group of publicly owned newspaper companies that withstood hostile attacks from hedge funds (Gannett and Lee), such as making efforts to reduce their physical property (RQ3-B).

Rather than emphasizing a low P/E ratio, it is more accurate to assert that companies experiencing a dramatic change in P/E ratio performance are most likely to be targeted by hedge funds. Firstly, if companies can maintain a positive P/E ratio for several years, it is considered the ideal scenario. This signifies that they have garnered more confidence from regular stockholders, leading to a higher stock price (Maverick, 2021), as seen in the case of Lee. A sharp rise in P/E can indicate that the company's new strategies have heightened expectations in the stock market. Conversely, a sudden decrease suggests that the strategy did not meet the market's expectations. When such setbacks occur repeatedly, they erode investors' confidence, as observed in the cases of Tribune Publishing and McClatchy. This erosion of confidence may lead to even lower confidence, as people often say that the stock market celebrates good news but does not like surprises (Lee, 2021). For instance, presenting a consistently low P/E ratio, as exemplified by Gannett, although it may not inspire great confidence in the future among shareholders, also does not create unrealistic expectations and results in a surprisingly low stock price. In short, hedge funds are interested in a relatively low stock price, and companies experiencing a dramatic change in P/E ratio can potentially lead to that point eventually.

Although no obvious pattern was found in terms of free cash flow among the four newspaper companies, it is evident that they all made efforts to maintain a positive free cash flow. This is particularly noticeable when comparing their performance in operational income, derived from advertising and circulation. The operational income showed a steady decrease, while the performance in this area exhibited significant fluctuations, indicating that the cash flow is dependent on their ability to interact with the capital market (Fernando, 2023), both gains and losses.

Therefore, when no more regular institutional equities are willing to invest in these companies, accepting a hostile takeover by hedge funds might become the companies' only choice.

A significant large portion of employee-related tangible resources in the observed public newspaper companies. From a hedge fund perspective, this large portion represents an opportunity to achieve immediate profit returns by reducing the workforce and subsequently cutting expenses. Examining the data, this study fund that although all four newspaper companies sharply reduced their workforce and associated expenses by over half over the span of 16 years, employee-related expenses still constituted a substantial portion of the total operating costs. For instance, Gannett and Tribune Publishing allocated over one-third to these expenses, while Lee maintained a figure of over 42% in 2022. In contrast, McClatchy's allocation was comparatively lower, at 25%. Furthermore, both Tribune Publishing (61% & 49%) and McClatchy (81% & 72%) maintained similar rates of reduction in both employee count and expenses. On the other hand, Gannett exhibited a significantly different pattern with a 73% reduction in employees and a 33% reduction in expenses. However, this phenomenon might suggest that the remaining employees at Gannett received relatively more benefits compared to those at Tribune Publishing and McClatchy. It also likely indicates that Tribune and McClatchy targeted their more experienced journalists and employees for layoffs.

In terms of physical property-related tangible resources, another pattern has emerged that differs from employee-related resources. First, as introduced in the method, the cost value of these properties is expected to be significantly lower than their current market value if they were sold instead of maintained (Twin, 2021). Therefore, the portion of property-related resources cannot definitively determine how much money a hedge fund may obtain through simultaneous sales. Nevertheless, the remaining portion of property-related value at cost remains very high for the four newspaper companies, with all of them exceeding 10%. McClatchy, in particular, exceeds 22%, which can significantly contribute to the immediate profit return goal of hedge fund owners. Second, all four newspaper companies have implemented aggressive cost controls on their physical property-related resources, with each of them exceeding 70%.

Gannett, in fact, reduced its physical property cost value by as much as 88% over the 16-year period. However, Tribune Publishing has a different story. Although they also made intensive cuts to their physical resources, they acquired more land and buildings among other physical properties in recent years. Considering the differences between the newspapers that failed against the attacks by hedge funds (Tribune Publishing & McClatchy) and the ones that successfully defended against hedge fund attacks (Gannett & Lee), it becomes evident that maintaining a low portion of physical properties in the composition of fixed asset allocation (e.g., land and buildings), can hold a higher potential for survival.

Lastly, the recorded data makes it evident that corporate transactions serve as a trigger point for hedge funds to take action because during such moments, the company becomes even more vulnerable to external attacks and influences. All four newspaper companies experienced some extreme corporate transactions that led to hostile actions by hedge funds. For example, Lee Enterprises became a target for a hedge fund shortly after merging with BH media group in 2020 (Mullin, 2021). These transactions and/or activities cost money, generally leaving the company with fewer resources to fight off hostile takeover attempts. In short, public companies' corporate transactions present the opportunity that hedge funds need to take action.

In summary, based on the data collected from the annual reports of the four observed public newspaper companies from 2007 to 2022, the results can partially represent or at least serve as a warning for the entire public newspaper industry. Maintaining positive or at least stable performance on P/E ratios, striving for positive free cash flow, treating employees well, keeping a low proportion of land and buildings among fixed assets, and avoiding extreme corporate transaction strategies can increase the likelihood of resisting hedge funds' hostile attacks.

References

Fernando, J. (2023, July). Free Cash Flow (FCF): Formula to calculate and interpret it. *Investopedia*. https://www.investopedia.com/terms/f/freecashflow.asp

Lee, M. (2021, April). What is Property, Plant, and Equipment (PP&E)? *Investopedia*. https://www.investopedia.com/ask/answers/06/propertyplantequipment.asp

Maverick, J. B. (2021, October). What is the best measure of a company's financial health? *Investopedia*. https://www.investopedia.com/articles/investing/061916/what-best-measure-companys-financial-health.asp

Mullin, B. (2021, November). Lee enterprises enacts poison pill to guard against Alden takeover. *The Wall Street Journal*. https://www.wsj.com/articles/lee-enterprises-enacts-poison-pill-to-guard-against-alden-takeover-11637793121

Twin, A. (2021, April). What is replacement cost and how does it work? *Investopedia*. https://www.investopedia.com/terms/r/replacementcost.asp

7

Study Two: Results and Discussion
The Impacts of Hedge Fund Ownership on the Newspaper Media Management and the Role of Journalism

Abstract Based on the data analysis of the twenty one in-depth interviews, there is evidence that hedge fund ownership's aggressive harvesting actions present significant threats to the newspaper's journalism mission, management operational objectives, and notably diminish the role of value-based issues, as developed in the literature review.

Keywords Journalism professional value • Media social impacts • Public interests • Newsroom operational objectives • Young journalists mentoring

In total, 21 interview participants were recruited over three months, from November 2023 to January 2024. Ten of them are from newspapers in Tribune Publishing, and eleven are from newspapers in the McClatchy company. Regarding the positions of the 21 participants, 15 (71.4%) hold newsroom leadership or management roles, such as executive editor or managing editor. The remaining participants are senior or investigative reporters who also shoulder significant responsibilities within the newsroom, such as serving on the editorial board and being members of Pulitzer Prize-winning reporting teams. Additionally, 16 participants

(76.2%) have over 25 years of experience as professional journalists, while the remaining participants have over 10 years of experience. Their sophisticated insights and experience demonstrate a sufficient understanding of the organizational (owner) goals and operational objectives.

For example, some participants mentioned that "As an editorial page editor… I oversee all editorial board people," "I'm the executive editor in our newsroom…and my team includes reporters, editors, photographers, and others" or "I've spent 22 years in the newsroom, I'm responsible for all of the journalism content that we produce and staff management." As detailed by several participants:

> I've been a journalist since about 1993. I directly supervise both reporters and editors and audience staff.…in addition to that, for several platforms, I am making strategic decisions (regarding) our news coverage to maximize audience page view traffic.
>
> I've spent the past 20 years here. I am the top manager in the newsroom. So, I am not only responsible for all of the work that we produced and the hiring process, but also I act as the top representative of our organization in the community, dealing with members of the community.

According to the literature review, three research questions are planned to be explored in this study. Specifically, how media managers perceive the owners' expectations regarding newspaper missions (RQ5), the management struggles in operational objectives (RQ6), and the owners' beliefs in social impacts (RQ7).

Newspaper Mission (RQ5)

Participants were asked about two types of missions: one concerning journalism quality and the other related to profit-driven motivation. Both inquiries sought information about what they were communicated by their hedge fund owners. In other words, it explores how hedge fund owners perceive the mission of the newspaper companies they acquire.

In terms of the mission regarding journalism quality (RQ5-A), the overall perspective proposed by all participants was that their hedge fund owners were absent in this regard, but there were different attitudes toward it. Some participants argued that the hedge fund's complete invisibility on this issue caused many newsroom management to struggle, while others believed that the lack of presence from the hedge fund was beneficial for journalism autonomy.

For example, when asked about how hedge fund owners communicate and evaluate journalism quality in the newsroom, all participants responded immediately with statements such as "They don't care that much about it," "You never hear from the hedge fund," "There's never communication to us," "They have remained as a pretty strict wall that you can talk with," "They pay very, very minimal attention," and "From what I understand, they don't know about journalism." As a couple of participants described:

> We don't have any interaction with anyone at the hedge fund, for the most part. They are not involved in the day-to-day workings, nor do they give any direction on what to cover or provide any help or guidance on that front. There is no indication that they care at all about that. When they actually sent a couple of people to the newsroom, it was shortly after a round of layoffs.
>
> If there is someone evaluating performance and journalism quality, we don't hear about it…no one talks to us at all…They own so many newspapers, to be honest, I would say they have little idea what's going on about the differences among us.

Afterward, some participants elaborated on the negative impacts. For example, when journalism quality is measured by report depth, some participants stated, "We don't have enough reporters for any subjects, so there is an underdevelopment in many content areas," and "Hedge fund ownership turns newspaper journalism missions into a joke." A couple of participants also provided similar perspectives:

> Now all of the digital specialists have to write Q&A or other reporting tasks to pretend like we have a broad range of industry literacy….For

example, I know zero people in (market) who are business leaders, but every week I have to write a story about that business profile kind of thing because they (hedge fund) hollowed out the business section....I have no idea what I'm writing.

I don't have a sense of what they (hedge fund owners) want...I don't think they know what we're doing day to day...they only pay attention to the page views metrics... I don't even know who's making the decisions to design those metrics to supervise our work.

However, some participants hold a positive perspective regarding the absence of hedge fund owners concerning newspaper journalism quality. As some participants indicated, "our hedge fund ownership has been pretty hands off" and "It's up to us to decide ultimately." For example, as a participant who is from McClatchy stated:

We really don't feel their influence on the quality of the content (we produce)...I believe it seems they respect what we're doing...Part of the reason is we underwent an entire journalism struggle (news staff shortage) when we were close to bankruptcy. After that, with the new hedge fund owners, although there hasn't been significant positive change, things haven't gotten worse.

Moreover, a participant who is from Tribune Publishing stated:

We haven't had much communication from Alden at all. However, at the newsroom level, our editors and managers consistently generate a reasonable stream of news stories, photos, and similar content each week. We have regular meetings and are largely self-motivated, I would say.

In terms of the profit-driven motivation mission (RQ5-B), the overall perspective regarding their hedge fund owners are entirely opposite when compared with the complete absence of hedge fund owners in journalism quality. All participants stated that the hedge fund owners intensely cares about profit return and routinely works with them on it. However, when asked about how hedge fund owners communicate and evaluate profit-driven motivation in the newsroom, participants from Tribune Publishing and McClatchy responded slightly differently. Tribune Publishing (Alden

Global Capital) focuses more on cost control, while McClatchy (Chatham Asset Management) emphasizes earning more.

For example, as participants from Tribune Publishing stated, they commonly receive messages about cost control, even though their hedge fund owners rarely communicate with them directly, as they observe what happens around them. As some participants pointed out, "there was very little like communication with us about how Alden was thinking (profit-driven)," "I think their mentality is simply to try to do things as cheaply as possible in order to make money," "Alden doesn't come to talk to us about profits…we're not included in those conversations… All we know is whether jobs get filled or remain vacant," and "We don't know if it's because of Alden, but we haven't had pay raises in a long time." As several participants described in detail, the hedge fund owners have implemented aggressive cost control measures, including controlling operational expenses, cutting employee benefits, and selling off physical resources:

> We're expected to meet our budgeted expenses every month, which can be challenging for journalists because we can't predict the news very well….In journalism, unexpected events occur a lot, such as hurricanes, which require extensive reporting and incur additional expenses. These occurrences are unpredictable within a month-to-month budgeting system…. Another important thing, if we save on expenses for a month and it doesn't roll over, it doesn't mean that next month we can spend a little bit more. That money is just gone!
>
> By labor law, they can't lay off union members. However, if a union member decides to resign, they don't have to fill the position…This aligns with their cost-control strategy… They have various methods to force people to leave without severance pay, such as cutting employee 401K matches for everybody, which are considered part of our salary.

Compared with a focus on cost control, participants from McClatchy have reported more direct communication from their hedge fund owners and a greater emphasis on increasing earnings, such as "They just want their money every month to pay the debt," "…As they are really trying to stabilize their profit… we have regular calls with them for updates on everything," and "We need to work with the online subscription metrics daily," and "The metric is designed to guide news product strategies to increase online paid subscriptions." As several participants described in detail:

> As far as I can tell, our owner asks us to focus on online subscription engagement…generating stories that engage readers and keep them on our site for as long as possible…Within these stories, we provide choices for related content or stories that perform well, driving more readership and profit.
>
> (The hedge fund owner) uses various metrics to track our reader engagement…They may ask us to cut a certain content category if it doesn't align with readers' interests (spend more time on those pages). For instance, readers may tell us (editors) that certain content is informative, but if they don't engage in paid activities (as recorded by metrics), we may have to make cuts.

In summary, the interview data reveals that hedge fund owners do not prioritize the mission of journalism quality; instead, they extensively emphasize profit-driven motivation. The complete lack of interest in journalism quality manifests in different attitudes among participants. Some participants blame the owners' absence for the decline in journalism quality, while others credit the hands-off approach of owners for providing more room for them to fulfill the journalism mission in the newsroom.

Operational Objectives (RQ6)

According to the literature review, this research question encompasses two main objectives through the lens of organizational resource support: the training of young journalists and the management of overwhelming workload. In other words, under full governance by hedge funds, what challenges do media managers face when navigating those operational objectives?

At the beginning, participants were asked a general question to describe the impacts of their hedge fund owners on the management work landscape, particularly focusing on daily reporting tasks such as news coverage and news beats. All participants pointed out that the shortage of news employees and limited organizational resources are the major impacts. For example, regarding the shortage of journalists, participants indicated, "It is in (market), we used to have around twenty (beat specific) reporters here, but now we only have one," "We only have one city hall reporter who covers (multiple) cities, including (one very large) city, which has a population of one million," and "They don't get involved in our coverage or news reporting, but they cut back on travel expenses, leaving us with nowhere to go." There are more examples as stated by the participants.

> They cut all kinds of incremental spending. For example, when we need to conduct an investigation that requires purchasing documents from the government, it can get expensive. Governments often charge hundreds to thousands of dollars for these documents, and we (journalists) often don't know what's in them until we see them. However, these expense requests are easily cut by hedge fund owners now due to the low return on investment.
>
> I feel that we should have reporters present at important events like presidential races or sports games. However, what we hear from the hedge fund owners is that, 'we need to watch our travel budget,' or 'Why not watch the events on TV and write from home?' That has definitely affected news coverage over the last few years under hedge fund ownership.

The physical working space is another diminishing organizational resource that negatively affects the entire newsroom's working landscape. However, as many participants stated, it's difficult to attribute all of the shrinking resources solely to hedge fund ownership; the pandemic has also contributed to this issue. For example, "We lost our newsroom during COVID" and "During the pandemic, they moved us to a 'broom closet,' where we only have two desks and no windows." Some participants indicated that these changes were indeed due to their new hedge fund owners. For instance, one participant mentioned that their suburban newsroom had been sold by the hedge fund in recent months, stating, "We don't know where we're going, and they (the hedge fund owners) don't care." On the other hand, some participants hold an opposite opinion, suggesting that the shrinking physical resources were solely because of the pandemic. For instance, a participant stated that a small meeting place had been recently reopened, saying, "We've reopened it for two and a half months. It's a small room for about 6 to 8 people."

In summary, the massive departure of experienced news staff and the disappearance of physical newsrooms are the two major impacts on their daily reporting tasks. Based on the perspectives of interview participants, hedge fund owners should take full responsibility for the shortage of experienced human resources, and some responsibility for the depletion of physical resources, particularly in the newsrooms.

The Training of Young Journalists (RQ6-A)

In the interview participants' viewpoints, the management objective of training young journalists is a broader objective that reflects how the company treats its young hires and builds their career paths, and the overall feedback was pessimistic. Under hedge fund ownership, when some senior positions opened, young journalists are often hired primarily instead of the experienced ones who meet the job requirements, and the young ones are often treated very poorly. As many participants shared the viewpoint "because the owner perceives they (young journalists) are cheap." Some participants stated, "They (hedge fund owners) mostly hired really young people," and "I don't want to say immediate college graduates but pretty close to young twenties." Moreover, participants highlighted several approaches indicating that young journalists have not been treated well, such as receiving different job contracts with lower benefits, lacking formal training, and experiencing high turnover rates.

Regarding the issue of different job contracts, although the existing contracts have many problems that need to be solved, such as no raises under hedge fund ownership, they still provide acceptable protections for those hired before hedge funds took ownership. For instance, some participants stated, "We're still in negotiations for our first contract for years, without an agreement, they (the hedge fund owner) cannot lay me off" and "We have to negotiate every year for healthcare coverage." However, for those hired after the acquisition, job contracts lack sufficient protection. One participant, hired after hedge fund ownership began, has spent 5–6 years in the newsroom as a senior editor, as they mentioned:

> There are people who have old contracts with the company and have been around forever; they have pretty decent salaries and many vacation days, unlike us. Our contract has already given away some of the benefits that longer-tenured employees had.
>
> I contribute to my own 401(k), but they (hedge fund owners) don't match it at all. As for health insurance, they only pay about two-thirds of the premium. It's a really bad plan with a high deductible. Once I went to the doctor, I got warned, and the doctor asked me if I'm sure I want to proceed with the appointment and pay at that moment with such a poor plan.

In terms of the lack of formal training, this issue encompasses various aspects as participants pointed out. The main contributing factor is the mass departure of experienced news staff members caused by hedge fund ownership. The remaining senior employees are burdened with additional job tasks, leaving insufficient energy and time to provide training support. For instance, as a couple participants stated:

> You just don't have the time to work with them anymore. You can say, 'Hey, if you get a chance, look at the story I edited and see the changes that I made, and if you have any questions, don't hesitate to ask, either in an email or by calling me'….. And they've got to be out the next day to cover the next day's event, and it's just this snowball effect. It's unfortunate that this has now become the norm…..
>
> It's just about the volume of people. We are losing veteran reporters who have a vast body of knowledge. So, while we're hiring younger reporters who are very intelligent, dedicated, and smart, it's still very hard for them to match the output of a veteran who has been working in the field for 10 or 15 years…. However, we've had to take on the workload of three to four people, leaving us with not much time to maintain contact and communication with young hires.

Another contributing factor is the reduction of resources allocated to the training process for new hires, including systematic mentoring programs and funding. For instance, as several participants stated:

> The hedge fund mostly hires young people who lack formal training and mentorship. There is no formal training or mentorship program in place, and there is really no one helping them. They (young journalists) don't know the people in their new reporting environment, how the government works, or how the agencies operate.
>
> You could ask people, and everybody was willing to help you, but there is no structured mentoring program in place. I worry, especially since many of the new hires are really young, some fresh out of college…. It's just a slower rate of development. Whereas it may have taken three to five years to become an expert with good training as it used to, now it might take seven more years….

Additionally, hedge fund owners do not set expectations for younger hires; they are hired solely to fill positions with low pay. For instance, as some participants stated:

> It's kind of like if you're doing good work, they (the hedge fund owners) are happy to have you there because, honestly, they pay so little that they're just happy to have people willing to.
>
> So, you (the hedge fund owners) send these people (young hires), who have completely different subject expertise in something else, to cover stories that they shouldn't be covering. Do you just need a warm body?

Lastly, the diminishing physical workspace and transition to remote work environments also contribute to the challenges of training young journalists, a situation influenced by both hedge fund owners and the pandemic. For instance, as a couple of participants stated:

> During the pandemic, many of the longer-term reporters don't want to come into the office now. However, for our younger journalists, that's really difficult because they don't get that kind of experience from sitting next to the more experienced journalists and hearing how they ask questions…

> They miss out on the opportunity to quickly ask questions or receive guidance. This has also affected our management…Since we're not physically present, things that would have been easier to just say, 'hey, here look at this or let me show you this.'

Regarding the issue of high turnover rates, this factor also affects the newsroom's routine for jobs and management. Obviously, in addition to the departure of experienced news staff, the high turnover rates among young journalists present even more challenges for the remaining staff. They must constantly train and adapt to working with new people or temporarily take on the workload of two or three individuals. For instance, as a participant stated regarding the management struggle.

> Most of our breaking and local teams consist of new reporters who have been hired within the last three years. While we have senior staff members, there's a noticeable absence of mid-level employees. Many of the younger hires tend to leave after around three years, and we've even had individuals depart within less than a year…… For those of us who remain, a major challenge is the constant worry about suddenly being assigned more tasks, whether we are available or not.

However, for young journalists, the staff shortage creates more job opportunities, allowing them to quickly gain experience and enhance their resumes. This can facilitate them finding another job with better pay in the near future. For instance, some participants stated a positive attitude regarding high turnover rates.

A lot of young people, I think they really want to work in journalism, so they'll take on any task you ask them to do, they'll work really quickly to gain a lot of experience. Then, it's easy for them to apply to other jobs and get better pay afterward.

Due to staff shortages, young people are assuming responsibilities more quickly now. This situation is advantageous for young reporters as they handle significant tasks early in their careers….If they feel financially constrained and cannot afford marriage or homeownership with their current low-paying job, they may readily and easily seek better opportunities elsewhere to achieve their life goals.

In summary, the clear issue emerged here is the lack of a formal training process for young journalists, who are primarily hired by hedge fund owners solely because they are 'cheap.' Moreover, due to poor job contracts with low employee benefits, the turnover rate of young hires is high, which further exacerbates management struggles in daily reporting tasks. However, an interesting aspect also emerged: young journalists may find it easier to find jobs in hedge fund-owned newspaper companies, although they lack support from mentors.

The Overwhelming Workload (RQ6-B)

The mass exodus of experienced staff has presented a significant challenge. As a result, remaining staff members are compelled to take on multiple roles. However, refilling these positions proves challenging as convincing hedge fund owners to prioritize job vacancies is difficult. Their primary focus is on maximizing profits and repaying debts incurred during the acquisition of the newspaper company. Consequently, they prefer to hire less experienced journalists at lower costs, burdening them with unreasonable workloads.

Regarding the difficulty in refilling positions and other organizational resource support, as several participants indicated:

> No, there are no plans that I've heard of to hire experienced reporters, especially for enterprise and investigative roles. More and more experienced ones have left. I remember just before the pandemic; it would be hard to fit them (investigative reporters) into a conference room. There were so many people. I remember you couldn't even find a chair at these meetings….But now, there are plenty of empty chairs in that conference room….
>
> We have far fewer people than we used to covering things. It's just about the volume of people….It's shrunk dramatically. So, the way it affects their management is they are stuck trying to fill holes in the Titanic, right?

Regarding the impossible amount of workload and potential solutions for this juggling situation, as several participants indicated:

It's very difficult to fill the jobs with experienced staff, so you end up turning to much younger journalists... Some roles need to rely on freelance or interns. We don't hire a lot of freelancers because freelance is an easy budget item to cut (by the hedge fund owners). We use college interns, and we often mention how proud our summer interns are of their experience.... And it's true because they are literally thrown into the water and just told to swim.

We are trying to establish a new structure where we can set up fundraising at the local level. For example, we received a generous amount of donations that enabled us to fund a (beat specific) reporter. It's difficult to convince local companies to support us because they're concerned about why they should give us their money if the hedge funds are just going to take it or whatever. So far, at least we have managed to secure funding for one local reporter.

In summary, the interview data reveals many management challenges in setting operational objectives under hedge fund governance, particularly concerning the training of young journalists, and coping with overwhelming workloads. First and foremost, hedge fund owners tend to hire cheap and less experienced young journalists to fill positions left vacant by experienced news staff. Without the guidance of senior colleagues, young hires have no direct means of acquiring working knowledge, such as the news sources and reporting network. Additionally, with hedge fund owners uninterested in content quality and personal growth, young hires quickly become overwhelmed with work, leading to high turnover rates. The shortage of experienced news staff, along with the lack of formal training for young journalists, contributes to the serious problem of overwhelming workloads. All newsroom employees are finding they are expected to do more work with fewer resources.

Social Impacts (RQ7)

Based on the literature review, this research question focuses on value-based issues and aims to explore how hedge fund ownership view and impacts them. These issues include journalism ethical standards, local community service, and the role of journalism in a democratic society.

During the era of public ownership, despite initial aggressive market-driven approaches and later financial pressures, these values were consistently recognized as essential by public newspaper owners. However, with a shift toward purely financial equity and short-term profit-driven motives, the permanent change in these values is pivotal.

Journalism Ethical Standards

Without exception, all participants expressed notable concerns when asked about this research question. For these three value-based issues, all participants immediately responded with comments such as "I don't have any belief that they care about that," "We don't really hear from the owner on that way," "We don't hear…If they do, we wouldn't know it," and "they are just somebody you could never see or talk to for these issues." However, participants shared different viewpoints and concerns regarding different value-based issues. For instance, they generally don't worry about journalism ethical standards, as they can rely on their strong personal beliefs to guide their work independently of the influence of hedge fund owners. As several participants indicated:

> We have our own journalism ethics standards, which were established by individuals and implemented with our previous owner. These standards have remained unchanged and were carried over from before…. independent of the hedge fund ownership.
>
> We have to stay self-motivated…it is our primary drive to stay in this job for decades. We entered journalism not for the money. While it's true that our hedge fund owners have never told us to do things in ethical ways, it's our bottom line.

Regarding the issue of journalism ethical standards, it is usually a broad concept recognized by news staff in the newspaper industry, encompassing various aspects such as content quality, news source collection, and more. However, professional financial entities like hedge funds purposefully disregard these standards entirely because they do not align with their goal of short-term profit returns. The positive aspect here is that all interview participants believe they do not require ownership support to maintain their belief in journalism ethics.

Local Community Service

When it comes to local community service, they are concerned about the diminishing coverage of local news and the lack of support for local resources. As several participants indicated:

> I think that puts what we do in jeopardy because there is a lot of work we need to do in covering our communities that isn't necessarily going to make money in the short term. We are leaving a lot of potential stories and a lot of community problems on the cutting room floor.
>
> What ends up being lost there is the long-term mission because we're focused entirely on short-term results. Making connections with your community, developing sources, and gaining loyalty from your readers are essential for becoming the go-to source for information, news, and connectivity in the community.

Regarding the issue of local community service, it is the most visible threat posed by hedge fund ownership, as indicated by the participants. With less media coverage for local news and information, fewer journalists being hired, and more job gaps remaining unfilled, the social impact of local community service becomes increasingly challenging under hedge fund ownership.

The Role of Journalism in a Democratic Society

Additionally, concerning the role of journalism in a democratic society, the major concern is the perceived lack of hope and the absence of a better alternative model. As several participants indicated:

> They (the hedge fund owners) are satisfied with what they're currently receiving from us. We've been informed that our company is capable of meeting profit targets, although we're not aware of what those targets are.

If the business environment becomes extremely challenging, they may resort to selling off parts of the company. I can certainly envision that happening in the near future. The building is on fire!

This lack of flexibility hampers our ability to react to news. For journalists, this is incredibly frustrating. We receive news tips from people seeking help or a voice, but we often have to turn them down due to staff shortages or budget cuts. This lack of flexibility is particularly challenging for journalists who are not motivated by money.

Regarding the issue of the role of journalism in a democratic society, the predominant sentiment among the participants' feedback is a sense of hopelessness for the future. The primary role of journalism in supporting a democratic society is to seek the truth and inform the residents by providing comprehensive and inclusive news and information. However, this becomes increasingly challenging to accomplish without the support of organizational resources, leading to a lack of optimism for the future.

In summary, for the RQ7, the interview data highlights the profound threat posed by hedge fund ownership to the foundational values of journalism. Operating purely as financial equity institutions with a focus on short-term profit, hedge funds prioritize shrinking newsroom sizes and reducing news coverage until every last drop of profit is squeezed. Consequently, while the remaining news staff may uphold their beliefs in journalistic professionalism and ethical standards, they lack the platform to enact them effectively. This invisibility to the local community hampers their role in supporting democratic society as a whole.

Discussion

Tribune Publishing and McClatchy are two large newspaper companies that were recently acquired by hedge funds, and the research population was intentionally recruited from these two companies, specifically targeting individuals holding leadership positions in the newsroom. This analysis reached the point of data saturation, ensuring no new views were overlooked after interviewing 12 or 13 out of the total 21 participants. Therefore, the results of the in-depth interview data analysis can shed light on the current state of the impacts of hedge fund ownership on newspaper media management in the U.S.

Based on the data analysis of the twenty one in-depth interviews, there is evidence that hedge fund ownership's aggressive harvesting actions present significant threats to the newspaper's journalism mission, management operational objectives, and notably diminish the role of value-based issues at Tribune Publishing and McClatchy. In the meantime, the data also show that management must align with the values and motivations of the owners (Drucker, 2008), although this sometimes causes struggles with operational objectives in their daily work and negative social impacts, as indicated in the literature review.

In terms of hedge funds' disproportionate focus on newspaper missions, the data analysis indicates that hedge fund ownership prioritizes profit-driven motivation over journalistic mission and shows no interest in maintaining journalism quality. In the context of hedge fund ownership, any actions that deviate from profit-driven goals are often viewed as self-interest and are required to be minimized (Bansal, 2013; Bratton, 2008), such as journalism mission.

According to the interview data, hedge fund owners usually track profit and revenue in a timely manner, ensure cash flow, and control costs at least monthly, with zero tolerance for budget overruns. However, hedge funds do not communicate to newspaper companies what their target profit margin is. As a result, newspaper employees have no idea how much budget they can expect, including for reporting costs and human resources spending, which keeps them in a constant state of tension, anxious about where the next dollar will come from. Another significant source of anxiety is that newspaper employees are unsure of where their efforts should be directed, as their new owners show no interest in their previous or existing job performance—journalism quality. These hedge fund owners only prioritize content that can bring in more page views and thus engage more paid subscribers without investing any extra resources. In fact, these anxieties reflect why hedge funds always pursue full control of the businesses they acquire. Generally speaking, hedge funds adopt a short-term profit return strategy with the intention of maximizing profit quickly (Andrew & Ayako, 2010; Morgenson & Rosner, 2023), but different hedge funds approach this in various ways. For example, as participants explored, Alden is focused on cost-cutting in Tribune Publishing, while Chatham is more interested in page views and increasing revenue in McClatchy. As some participants indicated, Tribune Publishing was acquired while still profitable, with a large number of employees and sufficient physical properties. This prompted its hedge fund owners to focus on cost control to increase profit margins. In contrast, McClatchy was acquired during bankruptcy, with few remaining tangible resources, leading its new hedge fund owners to prioritize increasing earnings.

In terms of the challenge in managing operational objectives in the newsroom, the data analysis indicates that hedge fund ownership creates substantial obstacles for newspaper leaders. Due to initial rounds of buyouts and layoffs, many experienced veteran reporters and editors left the newsroom, and the hedge fund either refuses or delays in refilling these positions. This creates tremendous difficulties for news coverage and overwhelming tasks for the remaining newsroom employees. Fewer employees have to take on more tasks, resulting in a deterioration in content quality, such as uncovered stories, insufficient reporters for breaking news, and a lack of backup journalists for in-depth reporting. The absence of veteran journalists also raises another issue: there is rarely enough time to support younger hires because individuals are often tasked with the workload of 3–4 people. Functioning as "money-spinning machines," hedge fund ownership often leads to extensive layoffs to cut costs and increase profit margins (Morgenson & Rosner, 2023).

Another management struggle caused by hedge fund ownership is the limitation of organizational resources. To improve short-term profit returns, hedge fund owners cut costs wherever possible (Andrew & Ayako, 2010), including freelancing and travel funds. This leaves the newsroom stuck in an operational quagmire, unable to maintain normal operations. The best option hedge fund owners allow is to hire less experienced journalists to fill work holes with extremely low pay and minimal benefits contracts, such as hiring a recent college graduate to cover government reports for seven cities without any assistance from senior journalists. In fact, young journalists in hedge fund-owned newspaper companies are treated more like disposable commodities—hired because they are inexpensive and easily laid off when no longer needed. One positive aspect is that young journalists can quickly gain experience in these companies because they are often deployed to various positions and reporting areas. As a result, they build a robust resume in a short time and can easily find better job opportunities somewhere. Additionally, the rapid loss of physical workspace is another unique aspect of hedge fund-owned newspaper companies, exacerbated by the pandemic, which has led to a dramatic shrinking of newsrooms, with many newspapers permanently losing their physical newsroom spaces.

In terms of the bleak outlook for the role of journalism in democracy within society, the data analysis indicates that hedge fund ownership may at least undermine the newspaper's role in journalism and profoundly impact democracy. Robust local journalism forms the foundation of democracy, and local newspapers serve as watchdogs for local governments and inform residents (Firmstone & Coleman, 2017). However, under hedge fund ownership, fewer and fewer local journalists remain, resulting in a diminished contribution to the future development of journalism. Many veteran journalists and editors have left the field, while the high turnover rate among young journalists persists. In addition, as expressed in the interview data, there is an inability to cover government meetings, lack of experienced journalists for investigative reporting, and little concern about developing relationships with the community, which all impact the effectiveness of the role of journalism in democratic society.

Furthermore, the data indicated that the shift in ownership from publicly traded companies to hedge fund ownership may pose another threat to the role of journalism in democracy—the transition of acquired public companies into private entities (Stulz, 2007). This transition brings more management difficulties because private companies are not obligated to undergo public scrutiny and notify employees of any strategic decisions (Balasubramanian & James, 2022).

In summary, according to the data, hedge fund ownership is most likely causing irreparable damage in the newspaper industry and the role of journalism in democracy due to their short-term profit-driven approach.

References

Andrew, M., & Ayako, Y. (2010). The economics of private equity funds. *The Review of Financial Studies, 3*, 26.

Balasubramanian, K., & James, M. (2022, November). What are the advantages and disadvantages of a company going public? *Investopedia.* https://www.investopedia.com/ask/answers/advantages-disadvantages-company-going-public/

Bansal, P. (2013). Inducing frame-breaking insights through qualitative research. *Corporate Governance: An International Review, 21*(2), 127–130.

Bratton, W. W. (2008). Private equity's three lessons for agency theory. *European Business Organization Law Review (EBOR), 9*(4), 509–533.

Drucker, P. (2008). Introduction: Management and managers defined; management as a social function and liberal art; knowledge is all. *Management*, 1–25.

Firmstone, J., & Coleman, S. (2017). The changing role of the local news media in enabling citizens to engage in local democracies. In *The Future of Journalism: In an Age of Digital Media and Economic Uncertainty* (pp. 445–455). Routledge.

Morgenson, G., & Rosner, J. (2023). *These are the plunderers: How private equity runs – And Wrecks – America*. Simon and Schuster.

Stulz, R. M. (2007). Hedge funds: Past, present, and future. *Journal of Economic Perspectives, 21*(2), 175–194.

8

Conclusion

Abstract These two studies in the research together provide a comprehensive picture of how hedge fund ownership impacts the newspaper industry and the democratic mission of journalism. Study One examined financial issues, while Study Two explored human issues, offering insights not only into why the newspaper industry became vulnerable to hedge fund attacks but also into the concurrent management struggles under full hedge fund governance, thus extending the threats to the role of journalism in democracy.

Keywords Hedge fund media ownership • Democratic society • Journalism norms • Media management • Future threats

Specifically, Study One focused on the factors that prompt hedge funds to take action and how they select target newspaper companies. Since hedge funds typically target public companies and engage in stock market activities (Morgenson & Rosner, 2023; Stulz, 2007), the research population of Study One consisted of annual reports from public newspaper companies that have experienced hedge fund attacks, including Tribune Publishing, McClatchy, Gannett, and Lee Enterprises. Overall, this was a longitudinal study spanning from 2007 to 2022, analyzing 55 annual reports from four newspaper companies over 16 years. Study Two dealt into the impacts of hedge fund ownership on media management through the lens of managing knowledge workers (Drucker, 2008), examining how their harvesting strategy challenges media management practices, and exploring potential threats to the role of journalism in a democratic society. To ensure comprehensive results, this study conducted in-depth interviews, targeting individuals in management positions at newspapers acquired by hedge funds, namely Tribune Publishing (acquired by Alden in 2021) and McClatchy (acquired by Chatham in 2019). A total of 21 participants were successfully recruited, and the data showed saturation, indicating that no more new viewpoints emerged.

In the data analysis of Study One, several financial factors have been examined, based on the literature review. To achieve maximum profit return, hedge funds typically target undervalued public companies and wait for an opportunity when the stock price is relatively low (Barnier, 2021; Maverick, 2021), indicating that other common equity firms are not interested but the companies still possess strong asset liquidity (French, 2022; Phan, 2021). Sudden corporate transactions serve as signals for hedge funds to act (Stulz, 2007). Therefore, factors of P/E ratio (Fernando, 2021), free cash flow (Murphy, 2023), tangible resources (Morgenson & Rosner, 2023), and corporate transactions (Stulz, 2007), were examined to understand how publicly traded newspaper companies lose the confidence of normal equity firms in the stock market and attract hedge funds.

Factors such as P/E ratio and free cash flow can explain why traditional equity firms lost interest in the newspaper companies in the stock market. Noticeably, previous studies have indicated that a low P/E ratio suggests undervaluation and discourages future investment (Fernando, 2021; Simpson, 2021). However, Study One revealed that a dramatic change in the P/E ratio, whether high or low, raises questions among shareholders about the company's investment worthiness and increasing stock risks. This is because the two newspaper companies that successfully resisted hedge fund' attacks both shared a relatively steady and low P/E ratio, while the two hedge fund-owned companies exhibited a dramatically changeable P/E ratio in the little more than a decade before they were acquired. Struggling to maintain a positive performance in free cash flow was observed among the four newspaper companies studied, all of which experienced many years with substantial deficits. This indicates a general loss of capability in the capital market. Persistent poor performance in free cash flow suggests weak financial management or challenges in securing capital support (Murphy, 2023).

Another two factors of tangible resources and corporate transactions can explain the purpose and signal of hedge funds' hostile attacks on certain newspaper companies. First, after decades of development, all four observed newspaper companies still possess a substantial amount of tangible assets despite their continuous aggressive cost reduction efforts, as revealed in this longitudinal study. These assets typically include human and physical resources (Massey, 2016). Hedge funds are driven by the pursuit of short-term profit returns, and mining from tangible resources is considered the most efficient way (Morgenson & Rosner, 2023; Stulz, 2007). However, according to the data analysis of this longitudinal study, it appears that newspaper companies can potentially reduce attention from hedge funds by strategically consolidating their tangible resources. For example, Gannett and Lee have diligently cut costs and controlled spending on their physical resources, including buildings and lands. In contrast, there was no clear evidence to suggest that Tribune Publishing and McClatchy had similar considerations in their cost control strategy. Instead, they appeared to cut various resources indiscriminately in pursuit of short-term cash flow. In other words, according to the data analysis of this study, the reduction of tangible resources is aimed at ensuring greater sustainability in the market, as well as striving for competitiveness.

Second, extreme corporate transactions serve as a clear signal for hedge funds' attraction, which include spin-offs, mergers, and bankruptcies, as these represent vulnerable moments for publicly traded companies (Stulz, 2007). Data analysis revealed that nearly all extreme corporate transactions were linked to instances of hedge fund hostile attacks. For example, Tribune Publishing, once a healthy and profitable company, faced turmoil when its board chairperson departed and sold his entire 25% stake to Alden, purportedly in retaliation for his resignation (Davidow, 2020). Subsequently, Alden rapidly acquired additional shares from the stock market, swiftly assuming ownership of Tribune Publishing almost overnight (Coppins, 2021). An upcoming significant transaction among these four newspaper companies, as indicated by the data, is Gannett's one billion indebtedness due in 2027 (Gannett Annual Report, 2022). There is no evidence in the annual report data that shows Gannett may face additional attempts at hostile takeovers, but it does show a substantial financial pressure to meet this debt. In essence, staying vigilant about extreme corporate transactions is a strategy to avoid falling prey to hedge fund harvesting.

Study Two's in-depth interview data analysis provided meaningful human insights regarding the impacts of hedge fund ownership on newspaper management, further extending to the role of journalism in democracy. As participants stated, hedge funds do not actively participate in the day-to-day operations of the newsroom, leaving journalism decisions and content primarily to news managers. However, hedge funds' aggressive requirements on profit margins and full control of tangible resources (Acharya et al., 2013; Kahan & Rock, 2017), inevitably lead to management struggles in newspaper companies regarding existing journalism values and job performance. The factors examined in this study include mission, operational objectives, and social impacts, guided by Drucker's (2008) theoretical viewpoints regarding managing knowledge workers.

First, hedge funds, as asset management agency (Stulz, 2007), display no interest in the sustainability of the companies they acquire. Instead, they view these companies solely as entities with tangible assets to exploit quickly (Morgenson & Rosner, 2023; Stulz, 2007). As revealed by this in-depth interview data analysis, when hedge funds take ownership of newspapers, they disregard any intangible assets, such as journalism missions, while highly concentrating on profit-driven motives. All participants indicated that hedge fund ownership is entirely absent when it comes to focusing on the mission of journalism quality but is pervasive in areas related to profit return motivation, including cost control, and increasing earnings. This motivation is unlike the profit-driven motivation recognized in the era of public newspaper ownership, which aligns with journalistic values, focusing on maintaining journalistic independence and the belief that high-quality journalism is a competitive advantage (Lacy et al., 1996). For example, many participants mentioned that hedge fund owners exclusively focus on budget cuts, such as slashing the travel fund, without any consideration for content quality. Additionally, they reduce staffing to minimal levels, such as leaving only one local reporter to cover seven more cities without adequately considering geographic coverage.

Second, concerning the management struggles imposed by hedge funds on operational objectives, challenges arise in training young hires (Blatchford, 2021) and managing overwhelming workloads (Sylvie & Gade, 2009). For instance, due to poorly treated employee benefits, experienced journalists are forced to leave in search of better-paying jobs, leading to a mass exodus of experienced employees. Without an adequate number of veteran news staff, maintaining news coverage, content quality, and young journalist training becomes challenging. Furthermore, while it is difficult to persuade hedge fund owners to fill vacant positions left by departing employees, young journalists due to their cost-effectiveness usually fill the limited open positions. With no assistance from senior staff and poor contractual benefits, high turnover rates are prevalent among these young hires, with few staying in their positions for more than three years.

Third, and the most important, these phenomena above could lead to irreversible damage to the foundation of journalism in democracy. Three value-based issues were examined in the Study Two, which are journalism professional value, local community service, and the role of journalism in democracy. According to the data analysis, the first issue has not been challenged by hedge fund ownership because it pertains to journalistic ethical standards that individuals are trained in school and personally uphold. As explained in the literature review, news media managers often have a professional journalism identity that aligns closely with these ethical standards (Gade, 2008; Merrill, 1974; Siebert et al., 1963). Even so, without adequate financial and organizational resource support, these journalistic ethical standards may be compromised. As participants explained, reporting flexibility has been largely limited due to the scarce travel funding support and unfilled reporting positions. In contrast, the issues of local community service and the role of journalism have been significantly affected by hedge fund ownership. The values of local community service and the role of journalism in a democracy both align with the function of journalistic norms, which involves providing information and public service to the communities they serve (Merrill, 2012; Siebert et al., 1963). Most newspapers owned by hedge funds are local newspapers, and they have aggressively reduced the number of local reporters and editors, and close physical workplaces. As many participants indicated, limited media coverage for local news, including local government institutions and civil life, makes it difficult to maintain a true democracy.

In addition, Drucker's theory (2008) on knowledge worker management provides a framework for guiding the variables and research questions of this study, but it does not clearly indicate the impacts when the owner comes from outside the organization with extreme motivations that may conflict with the organization's initial values. While outside investors are not a new concept, most investors historically have been stockholders who exercised influence through participation on the corporation's board of directors, seeking long-term and stable profit returns (Lacy & Blanchard, 2003; McManus, 1994; Picard & Van Weezel, 2008). In contrast, hedge funds typically seek to gain full control of the companies they target, which may reflect an extreme form of outside ownership, extending Drucker's theory of knowledge worker management.

By examining these two studies holistically, several findings emerged that contribute to the existing literature in this field. One recommendation is to reduce the asset value of physical properties to avoid attracting hedge funds' interest. Another finding concerns the relationship between investing in employee benefits and enhancing competitiveness. The financial data from Study One indicated that newspaper companies have invested more in their remaining employees. However, Study Two showed that employee benefits were likely protected by the union, which helped fend potential layoff issues. The last finding is a two-edged idea: younger journalists might find more opportunities in hedge fund-owned newspaper companies due to their low entry-level employment benefits. However, they are also likely to become frustrated by the workload, newsroom environment, and lack of resources, leading them to move on to other papers. This turnover limits their relationship with their communities and readers.

This book sheds light on the relationship between ownership and media management, particularly focusing on the impacts of hedge fund ownership in journalism. While the effects of hedge fund ownership have

8 Conclusion

been studied across various industries, they have not been systematically examined in the field of journalism. The hedge fund industry experienced rapid growth in recent business history, especially following the 2008 recession (Clarke, 2024). Previous studies have explored their influence in other sectors, such as real estate and nursing homes. Although their involvement in journalism began around 2010, it gained significant public attention with the acquisition of Tribune Publishing by Alden Global Capital in 2021 (Coppins, 2021). However, prior to this book, there has been limited research in this area. Furthermore, this book represents the first attempt to utilize financial analysis methods and financial data for analysis in the field of journalism, including metrics like P/E ratio and free cash flow. Additionally, this series of in-depth surveys delve into media management issues, focusing exclusively on newsroom leadership within hedge fund-owned newspaper companies. It offers a comprehensive snapshot of the media landscape, providing valuable perspectives for newspaper companies potentially facing threats from hostile hedge fund takeovers. These threats include the departure of experienced journalists, high turnover rates among young journalists, overwhelming and low-quality content production, and staff shortages in local community service, all of which contribute to the erosion of the foundation of journalism's role in democracy.

While this book has several limitations, it also inspires numerous potential avenues for future research that warrant exploration. For example, by relying primarily on annual reports, many of the critical incidents and their impact on the companies in period prior to hedge fund ownership are missed and not considered (e.g., sales of properties, layoffs, contract negotiations and employee concessions). Hence, some companies do not sufficiently maintain access to open resources, resulting in some missing annual reports. Thus, using paid resources from third-party independent financial analysis firms may be advisable for future studies, or combining more financial sources might add richness to the data. Moreover, because this book is the first attempt to apply financial analysis methods in the field of media studies, it required tremendous effort to identify and operationalize many financial terminologies from scratch. This includes determining how to identify correlated information such as operational revenue, net revenue, free cash flow, and capital revenue, as well as understanding their relationships when collecting data from annual reports. Further work may be necessary to differentiate between these various concepts when conducting cross-disciplinary research in the future.

Furthermore, recruiting participants proved challenging due to the sensitive nature of the topic for current managers in hedge fund-owned newspapers. Many individuals chose not to respond to the interview invitation letters, as several potential issues exist. For example, high-level managers may find it difficult to reach out to unfamiliar email addresses, particularly when discussing their current owners; union members may face pressure to remain silent during negotiations between unions and hedge fund owners.

Future studies may benefit from designing innovative methodologies that can closely observe the nuanced issues pertaining to hedge fund ownership of newspapers, moving beyond a sole focus on the threats to the newspaper industry and the role of journalism in democracy.

Overall, newspaper companies are facing numerous challenges in the digital era, such as the shift in audience reading habits, advertisers' dispersed advertising budgets, and the emergence of digital media competitors (Picard, 2011). The presence of hedge fund ownership may pose additional challenges to the newspaper industry, particularly concerning journalism quality and economic conditions. Therefore, it is important to examine more factors and the broader impacts of hedge fund ownership on the newspaper industry and journalism, especially as an increasing number of newspapers and media firms are being acquired by hedge funds.

References

Acharya, V. V., Gottschalg, O. F., Hahn, M., & Kehoe, C. (2013). Corporate governance and value creation: Evidence from private equity. *The Review of Financial Studies, 26*(2), 368–402.

Barnier, B. (2021). Hedge Fund. *Investopedia*. https://www.investopedia.com/terms/h/hedgefund.asp

Blatchford, T. (2021, August). How students and early career journalists can approach potential mentors with intention and respect. *Poynter*. https://www.poynter.org/educators-students/2021/how-students-and-early-career-journalists-can-approach-potential-mentors-with-intention-and-respect/

8 Conclusion

Brav, A., Jiang, W., Partnoy, F., & Thomas, R. (2008). Hedge fund activism, corporate governance, and firm performance. *The Journal of Finance, 63*(4), 1729–1775.

Chyi, H. I., & Ng, Y. M. M. (2020). Still unwilling to pay: An empirical analysis of 50 US newspapers' digital subscription results. *Digital Journalism, 8*(4), 526–547.

Clarke, C. (2024, February). Hedge fund definition, examples, types, and strategies. *Investopedia*. https://www.investopedia.com/terms/h/hedgefund.asp

Coppins, M. (2021, October). A secretive hedge fund is is gutting newsrooms. *The Atlantic*. https://www.theatlantic.com/magazine/archive/2021/11/alden-global-capital-killing-americas-newspapers/620171/

Davidow, S. (2020, May). The state of journalism at Tribune Publishing. *The NewsGuild*. https://newsguild.org/the-state-of-journalism-tribune-publishing/

Drucker, P. (2008). Introduction: Management and managers defined; management as a social function and liberal art; knowledge is all. *Management*, 1–25.

Fernando, J. (2021, November). Price-to-Earnings (P/E) ratio. *Investopedia*. https://www.investopedia.com/terms/p/price-earningsratio.asp

French, D. (2022, May). Hedge fund Elliott chases oil and gas deals, bucking Wall Street. *Reuters*. https://www.reuters.com/markets/us/hedge-fund-elliott-chases-oil-gas-deals-bucking-wall-street-2022-05-25/

Gade, P. J. (2008). Journalism guardians in a time of great change: Newspaper editors' perceived influence in integrated news organizations. *Journalism & Mass Communication Quarterly, 85*(2), 371–392.

Gannett Annual Report. (2022). *Gannett*. Retrieved from: https://s202.q4cdn.com/162862548/files/doc_financials/2022/ar/2022-annual-report.pdf

Hendrickson, E. M., & Subotin, A. (2023). Mergers, acquisitions and magazine media in 2021. *Journalism Practice, 17*(5), 1031–1045.

Hollifield, A. (2012). Changing perceptions of organizations. *Changing the news: The forces shaping journalism in uncertain times*, pp. 193–212.

Kahan, M., & Rock, E. B. (2017). Hedge funds in corporate governance and corporate control. In *Corporate Governance* (pp. 389–461). Gower.

Lacy, S., & Blanchard, A. (2003). The impact of public ownership, profits, and competition on number of newsroom employees and starting salaries in mid-sized daily newspapers. *Journalism & Mass Communication Quarterly, 80*(4), 949–968.

Lacy, S., Shaver, M. A., & Cyr, C. S. (1996). The effects of public ownership and newspaper competition on the financial performance of newspaper corporations: A replication and extension. *Journalism & Mass Communication Quarterly, 73*(2), 332–341.

Massey, B. L. (2016). Resource-based analysis of the survival of independent web-native news ventures. *Journalism & Mass Communication Quarterly, 93*(4), 770–788.

Maverick, J. B. (2021, October). What is the best measure of a company's financial health? *Investopedia*. https://www.investopedia.com/articles/investing/061916/what-best-measure-companys-financial-health.asp

McManus, J. H. (1994). *Market-driven journalism: Let the citizen beware?* Sage Publications.

Merrill, J. C. (1974). *The imperative of freedom: A philosophy of journalistic autonomy*. Hastings House.

Merrill, J. C. (2012). Journalism and democracy. In *Changing the News* (pp. 45–62). Routledge.

Morgenson, G., & Rosner, J. (2023). *These are the plunderers: How private equity runs – And Wrecks – America*. Simon and Schuster.

Murphy, C. (2023, May). Using the price to earnings ratio and PEG to assess a stock. *Investopedia*. https://www.investopedia.com/investing/use-pe-ratio-and-peg-to-tell-stocks-future/

Noam, E. (2009). *Media ownership and concentration in America*. Oxford University Press.

Noam, E. M. (2006, August). *Media concentration in American and the world*. TPRC.

Phan, T. T. (2021). A former hedge fund trader founded America's leading nonalcoholic craft beer. *Hustle*. https://thehustle.co/01202021-athletic-brewery-nonalcoholic/

Picard, R. G. (2010). The future of the news industry. *Media and Society, 5*, 365–379.

Picard, R. G. (2011). *Mapping digital media: Digitization and media business models*. Open Society Institute.

Picard, R. G., & Van Weezel, A. (2008). Capital and control: Consequences of different forms of newspaper ownership. *The International Journal on Media Management, 10*(1), 22–31.

Siebert, F. S., Peterson, T., & Schramm, W. (1963). *Four theories of the press*. University of Illinois Press.

Simpson, S. (2021, August). Low-risk vs. High-risk investments: What's the difference? *Investopedia*. https://www.investopedia.com/financial-edge/0512/low-vs.-high-risk-investments-for-beginners.aspx

Stulz, R. M. (2007). Hedge funds: Past, present, and future. *Journal of Economic Perspectives, 21*(2), 175–194.

Sylvie, G., & Gade, P. (2009). Changes in news work: Implications for newsroom managers. *Journal of Media Business Studies, 6*(1), 113–148.

Index

A

Abbott, A., 54, 61
Abernathy, P.M., 6, 7, 9
Acharya, V. V., 7, 158
Achleitner, A. K., 33, 36, 37, 39
Adam, B., 77
Adams, M. T., 10, 36
Albarran, A. B., 8, 20, 39, 51, 77
Alpert, L., 34
Amaded, K., 36
Andersson, U., 75, 78
Andrew, L., 24
Andrew, M., 78–81, 151, 152
Annual report, 4, 6, 11, 12, 94, 95, 97–104, 117, 118, 127, 129, 132, 155, 156, 158, 161, 162
Arsal, M., 35
Ayako, Y., 78–81, 151, 152
Ayash, B., 2, 79

B

Bagdikian, B. H., 21, 23, 39
Balasubramanian, K., 81, 153
Bansal, P., 7, 38, 80, 151
Barber, B., 55
Barnier, B., 20, 36, 156
Bary, A., 29
Bass, B. M., 10
Bass, J., 21, 24, 39
Beam, R. A., 2, 28, 29, 54, 55, 57, 59, 61, 71
Becker, L. B., 54–56, 58
Benderev, C., 106
Benson, R., 80, 81
Besemer, S. P., 77
Bhandari, S. B., 10, 36
Bharath, S. T., 37, 38
Blatchford, T., 69, 76, 159
Bloomenthal, A., 102

Blouin, J. L., 39
Boesman, J., 6
Boudoukh, J., 29
Bratton, W., 7, 80
Brav, A., 2, 34, 36, 38, 93
Breed, W., 23
Bryan, C. R., 20, 21, 24, 38, 40
Bryan, R., 7, 8
Buchanan, J., 38

C

Cagé, J., 30
Cameron, K. S., 70
Campbell, R., 23, 24
Carlson, B., 26
Carpenter, R. E., 29
Caruana, E. J., 11
Chadha, M., 29
Channick, R., 9, 20, 29, 32, 68, 76
Chan-Olmsted, S. M., 72, 80
Chasan, E., 32
Chen, J., 26, 101
Chiou, L., 30, 31
Christians, C. G., 38, 51, 52
Clarke, C., 2, 3, 7, 161
Coffee Jr, J. C., 37
Coppins, M., 1, 2, 20, 32, 34, 37, 38, 40, 50, 51, 58–60, 62, 68, 69, 76, 79, 81, 94, 97, 100, 158, 161

D

Dembek, K., 68, 72
Demers, D., 2, 3, 8, 9, 20–25, 27, 28, 31, 39, 40, 50, 58, 73–75, 78, 82, 107

Demsetz, H., 8
Denis, D. K., 27
Denzin, N. K., 11, 94, 104, 105
Depersio, G., 102
Dittmar, A., 35
Drucker, P., 4, 7, 8, 11, 68–72, 74, 76, 82, 83, 94, 104, 151, 156, 158, 160

E

Edmonds, R., 7, 10, 33, 37
Emery, E., 23, 25, 26
Escobar, N., 76, 108
Eveland Jr, W. P., 30

F

Fernando, J., 2, 3, 26, 39, 51, 100, 130, 156
Field, L. C., 35
French, D., 35, 156

G

Gad, S., 2
Gade, P. J., 4, 5, 9, 20, 25, 28, 29, 56, 59, 69, 73–77, 79, 82, 83, 159
Galbraith, J. K., 40
Garbaravicius, T., 36
Ghaeli, M. R., 10, 25, 35, 36
Ghaljaie, F., 106
Goli, H., 106
Goode, W. J., 54
Grundy, A., 57

H

Hall, K., 10, 34, 36, 59, 94, 97, 98
Hartzell, J. C., 12
Hawkins, D. I., 105
Hayes, A., 26, 94
Hemlin, S., 72
Herzberg, F., 71
Hess, T., 5, 30

J

James, M., 22, 81, 153
Josephi, B., 71

K

Kahan, M., 33, 34, 38, 158
Killebrew, K. C., 77, 108
Kramer, M. R., 71

L

La Merced, M., 31
Lacy, S., 2, 5, 9, 22, 25, 28, 29, 49, 50, 56–58, 62, 68, 75, 80, 83, 158, 160
Lavine, J. M., 28, 31
Lee, E., 34, 95, 96, 98, 117–127, 129, 130, 157
Lee, M., 131, 132
Leepsa, N. M., 9
Lindgreen, A., 68, 72, 73
Lindlof, T. R., 105
Lowrey, W., 5, 6, 8, 20, 28, 56, 59, 77
Luscombe, M., 25

M

Macey, J., 38
Maher, S., 20, 33
Matsa, K.E., 4
McCahery, J. A., 7
McDowell, W. S., 5
McManus, J. H., 29, 57, 58, 74, 160
McQuail, D., 55
McQuiston, J. T., 22
Merrill, J., 8, 19, 20, 28, 29, 73, 82, 160
Meyer, P., 8, 10, 20, 22, 28, 33, 37–39, 50, 74, 75
Mintzberg, H., 70
Moser, T., 111
Mythen, G., 56, 61

N

Nix, E., 5

O

O'Connell, J., 6, 9, 34
O'Connor, C., 6
O'Neill, D., 6
O'Quin, K., 77
Ori, R., 60

P

Palia, D., 37
Pew Research Center, 3, 4, 32
Phan, T. T., 35, 156
Picard, R. G., 2–6, 11, 20–24, 27–31, 33, 39, 40, 50, 56–58, 61, 68, 69, 73–78, 82, 83, 93, 94, 98, 108, 110, 160, 162

Powers, A., 22
Preston, P., 57

R
Riffe, D., 97
Rosenstiel, T., 21, 56, 73, 80
Rosenstiel, T. B., 23

S
Schmidt, J., 7
Schumpeter, J. A., 77
Schwoebel, J., 23, 24, 40
Scott, G., 81
Siebert, F., 9, 49–54, 60, 61
Simpson, S., 7, 156
Singer, J. B., 61
Snider, M., 96
Soloski, J., 2, 3, 27, 28, 31, 40, 75
Sonderman, J., 31
Stacey, R. D., 68, 72
Starks, L. T., 12
Streeck, W., 49
Stulz, R. M., 2, 3, 7, 9, 10, 12, 33, 36–38, 51, 59, 62, 69, 78–81, 83, 94, 99, 101, 108, 153, 155–158
Swayne, E. E., 23, 25, 27, 28, 39
Sydney, E., 20, 32
Sylvie, G., 20, 25, 69, 74, 75, 77, 82, 159

T
Tajpour, M., 22
Tameling, K., 9
Tenenboim, O., 11, 68, 76, 98
Tierney, W., 71
Topping, S., 26

Tretina, K., 7
Twin, A., 101, 131

U
Uhl-Bien, M., 77
Underwood, D., 22, 25, 27–29, 31, 57
Usher, N., 50, 59, 80

V
Van den Bulck, H., 6
Van der Burg, M., 6
Van Gorp, B., 6
Viaud, M. L., 30
Vlad, T., 54–56, 58

W
Walker, M., 4, 6
Watson, A., 76
Watson, B., 97
Weaver, D. H., 55, 56, 58, 80
Weir, C., 33
Wilensky, H. L., 56
Wilhoit, G. C., 55, 56, 58, 80
Williams, M., 111
Wohlner, R., 7
Wong, Y. T. F., 35
Woo, C. W., 6, 8
Wright, M., 33

Y
Yin, R. K., 104

Z
Zelizer, B., 56
Zucchi, K., 99, 100

Printed in the United States
by Baker & Taylor Publisher Services